In memory of Jim Duffy

ISBN 978-2-912393-26-5
© CMP Publishing 2012
PO box 1794-Dubois WY 82513
Contact E-mail : cp-courriere@orange.fr
Design by Hors-Série : Patrick Miramand

Wyoming from the air
where the eagle soars

Photography Claude Poulet
Text Bayard Fox

FOREWORD

Wyoming is that vast tract of high plains, badlands, plateaus, alpine meadows, meandering rivers and towering mountains that tens of thousands of Americans fly over annually on their way to the Left or Right coasts.

At 35,000 feet from the cabin of a Boeing 737, however, it is impossible to appreciate the remarkable topographical diversity and raw beauty which characterize our tenth largest and least populated state. Its landscape remains one that most of us in this country never truly see, experience or are able to appreciate.

There's no urban sprawl within Wyoming's borders, no pollutant pluming smoke stacks. This is where the Rocky Mountains meet the Great Plains. The high country abounds with great herds of elk, moose, mule and white tailed deer, grizzlies and black bear; the plains and the plateaus with antelope and enormous herds of cattle that were first brought to the region more than 150 years ago from Texas.

The state is home to great rivers and world class fisheries including the Snake, the North Platte and the Green. These waterways and the hundreds of other smaller rivers, stream and creeks in Wyoming are fed by the melting snows from the many mountain ranges that traverse the state. Among them : the Absarokas and Winds, the Big Horns, the Laramie Range that extends north from Colorado and, of course, the Tetons that soar to the south of Yellowstone Park, the crown jewel of our national parks.

The native people – the Crows, Shoshone, Northern Cheyenne and Arapahoe – viewed the region as their home for centuries, drawing upon seemingly endless herds of buffalo to sustain their existence. The mountain men and fur traders saw the areas profusion of beaver as a cash crop and a means of living unfettered lives beyond the reach of encroaching of civilization.

The early cattle ranchers, many of them English lords, quickly capitalized on the potential of the rich pasturelands in the Powder River Basin and along the Sweetwater. And the emigrants bound for Oregon and California saw Wyoming as the passage way to the promised land, following the Platte River and traversing the one level route through the Rocky Mountains, South Pass.

Visiting Wyoming from his native France for the first times in 1982, photographer Claude Poulet felt an immediate affinity for the region's seemingly endless vistas. Four years ago he did a book of Wyoming photographs in collaboration with Bayard Fox that was well received. More recently he began photographing Wyoming landmarks from the air all across Wyoming. The result, the first full blown portrait of the state from an eagle's eye view, or in this instance, an eagle eyed photographer "Wyoming from the Air; Where the Eagle Soars".

Laton McCartney

Devils Tower is one of the world's most striking topographical wonders, rising over 1,200 ft. almost straight up out of the surrounding land. It was the first place to be declared a United States National Monument and is one of Wyoming's most often visited tourist attractions receiving about 400,000 visitors a year. It is easy to understand why Native Americans revered this place for thousands of years before European explorers saw it. The tower is still sacred to the Indian tribes in the area which causes some conflicts with the many climbers for whom its steep cliffs offer an irresistible challenge. The Indians feel that the climbers profane the sanctity of this spiritual place and compromises have been required on both sides. Since June is the most sacred month for Indian ceremonies there is a voluntary ban on climbing that month. About 4,000 people a year make the climb which usually takes 4 or 5 hours. The record ascent was made by Todd Skinner climbing alone without ropes in only 18 minutes. At least five people have fallen to their deaths attempting to ascend or descend these steep cliffs.

Geologists cannot agree as to how this unique formation was produced though some feel that it is the neck of an extinct volcano. The derivation of its modern name in English was caused by an interpreter's mistranslation and something like "Grizzly Bear Lodge" would have been more appropriate. At least 20 different tribes have some affiliation with the Tower and each has a somewhat different legend to explain it. Many of the legends agree that the grooves in the rock were made by the claws of a giant grizzly.

Wyoming is home to one of the great natural treasures on our planet ; Yellowstone Park. It was the first national park preserved by any country and remains the most famous. Despite its remote location, it has about 3 million visitors a year. Signs of volcanic action are everywhere and the fiery tumult of the earth's interior is often close to the surface. Multiple geysers periodically spout huge quantities of steam and water into the air and there are thousands of ponds and springs where the water boils. Old Faithful consistently spews a spectacular plume over a hundred feet into the air every hour or so as it has done for unknown years.

Several waterfalls plunge hundreds of feet in steep, rainbow hued canyons. The Park straddles the Continental Divide and the many streams which rise here empty into both Atlantic and Pacific Oceans. There are hundreds of different species of animals, birds, reptiles and fish, several of which are very rare. The volcanic and glacial activity has created many large and small lakes often

The Grand Prismatic Spring is the largest hot spring in the United States

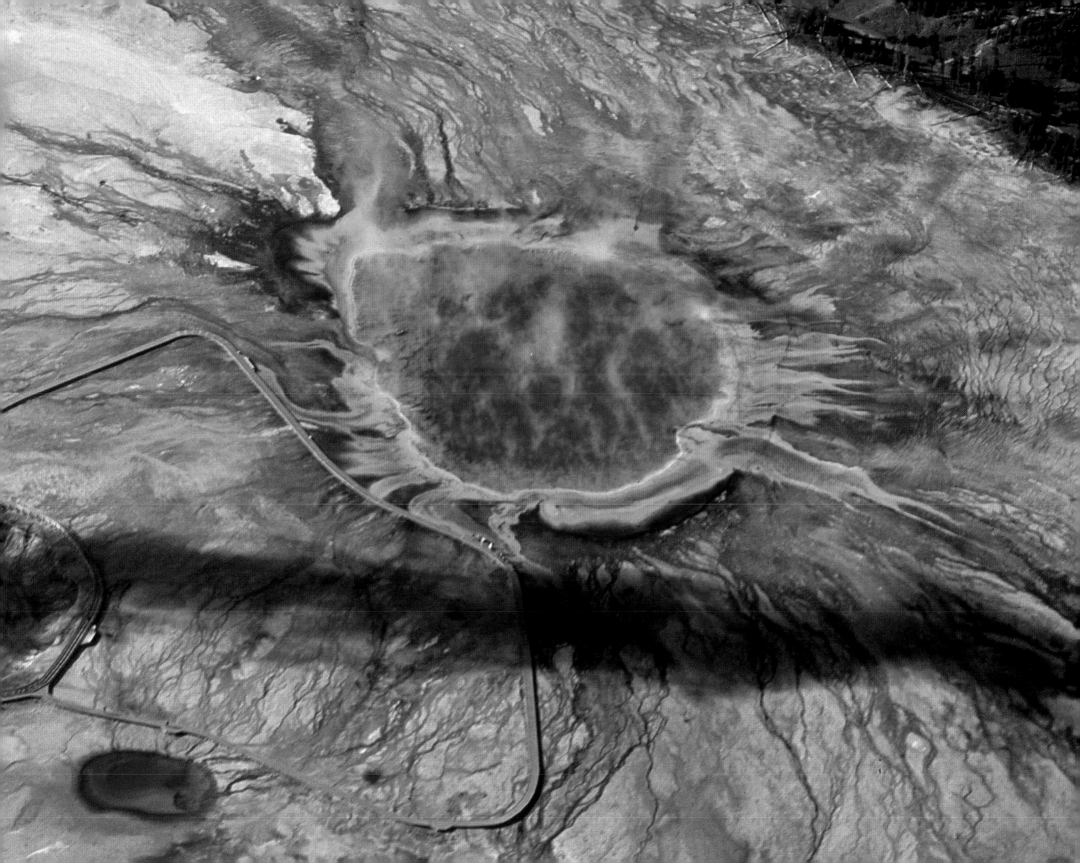

"The Lower Falls of the Yellowstone which drop twice the distance of Niagara Falls to the bottom of a breathtaking canyon are certainly one of the most awesome views to be found in North America.

Next page :
A herd of buffalo grazing peacefully along a little stream.

The wide delta of the Yellowstone where the River empties into the Lake.

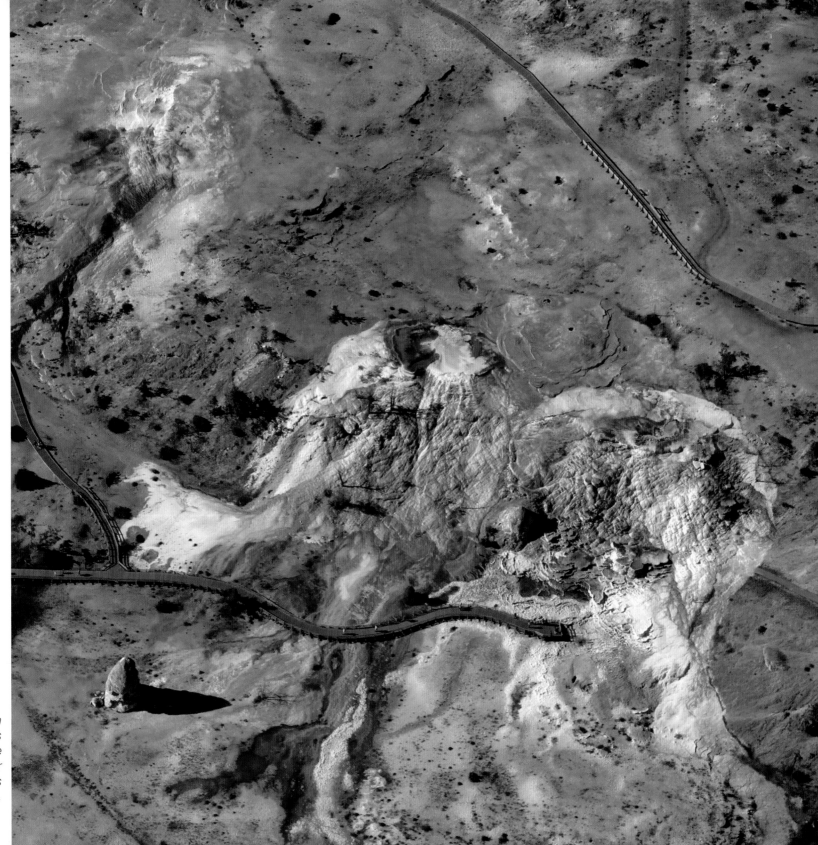

12

Mammoth Hot Springs is one of the most popular attractions of the Park.

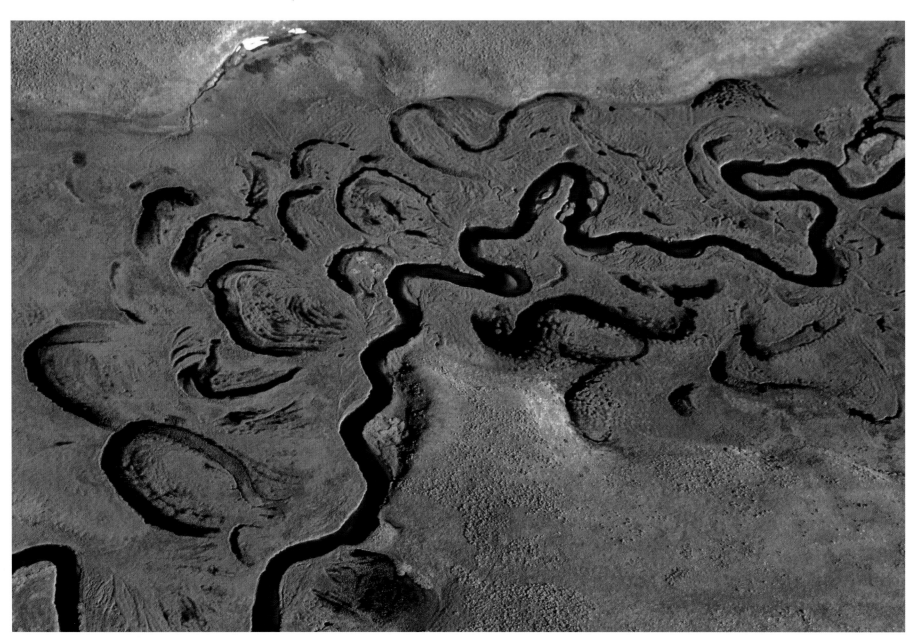

Over the millennia Pelican Creek has changed its course numerous times as it finds its torturous way toward Yellowstone Lake.

connected by streams which make excellent habitat for the native cutthroat trout, attracting people from round the world to fish in these pristine waters. Over 1,000 archeological sites of Native Americans dating back at least 11,000 years have been discovered. An obsidian cliff of exceptional quality in the Park has been mined for millennia by native tribes as it

elk, buffalo, deer, big horned sheep, grizzly bears and wolves can migrate freely over a wide area as in pre-Columbian days. It required tremendous foresight and courage on the part of our forefathers to preserve this unique system for the world to appreciate.

is ideal for making sharp stone tools and projectiles. This obsidian must have been widely traded as it has been found as far away as Mexico, Ohio and central Canada.

The Park itself is roughly half the size of New Jersey and forms the heart of the Greater Yellowstone Wild Ecosystem which is ten times larger and still preserves most of its wild character unspoiled by development. This wider system, made up mainly of surrounding national forests and parks, is the largest wild system left in the temperate zone of the northern hemisphere. Its significance is enormous because it is the only area left in this part of the world where wild game like

The Park was established in 1872 and in the early years little was done to prevent its exploitation by miners, poachers, settlers and lumbermen. There was considerable local pressure to open up the area for commercial development. The buffalo herds were being poached in their last refuge and the area was threatened by an ugly fate similar to Niagara Falls. Fortunately far sighted leaders like Ferdinand Hayden convinced Washington to allocate the resources necessary for protection of its unique wild beauty, minerals, flora and fauna. They have certainly been vindicated in their policy by millions of appreciative visitors from around the world.

Yellowstone Lake fills a large part of the caldera left by an ancient volcano.

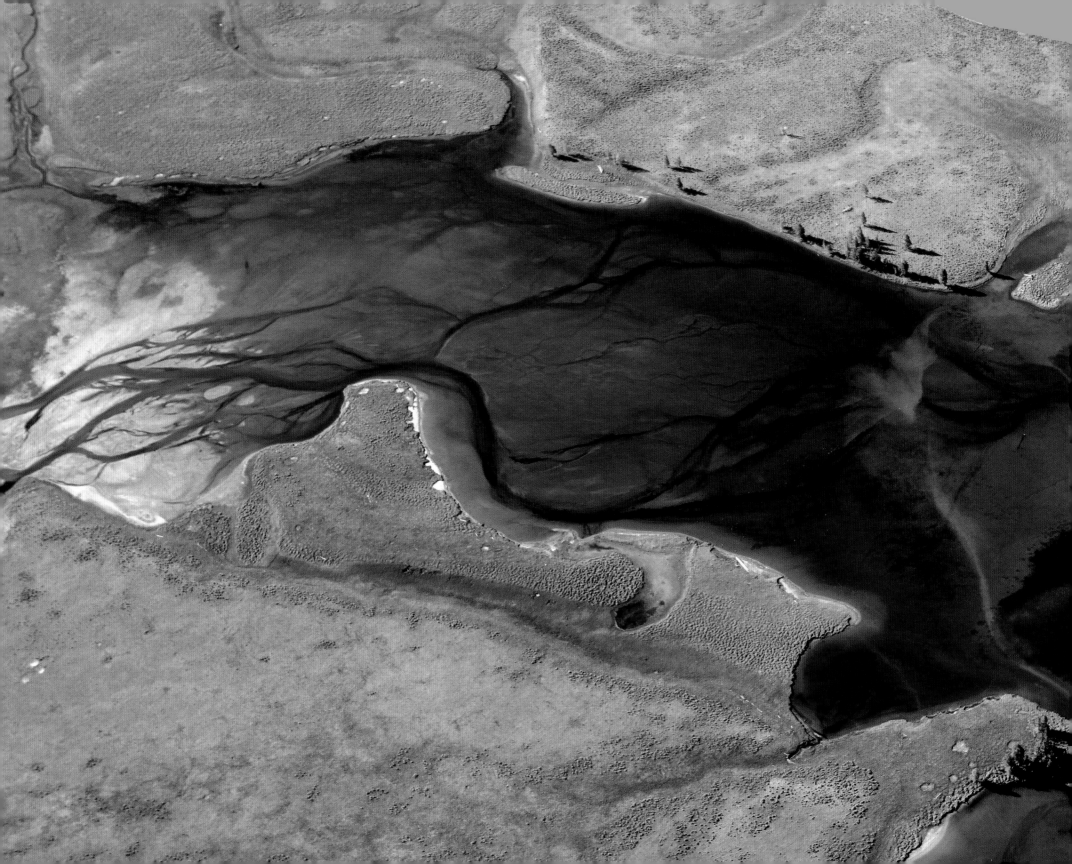

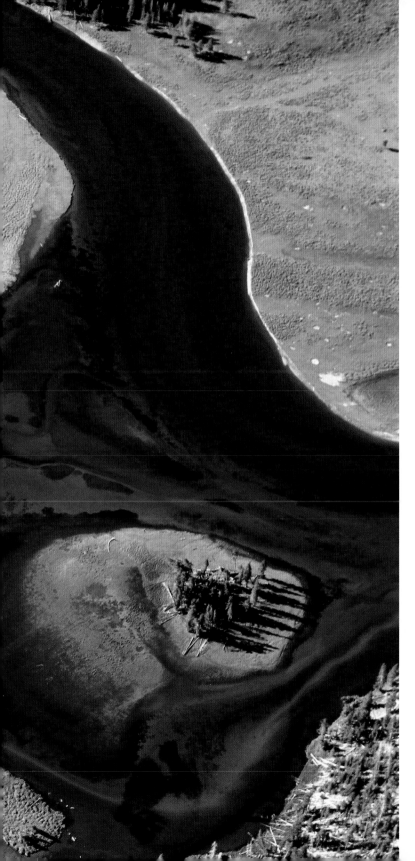

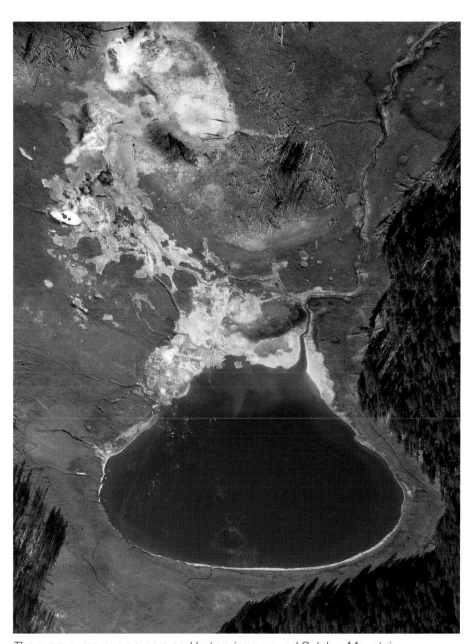

There are numerous geysers and hot springs around Sulphur Mountain.

The Yellowstone River passes majestically through Hayden Valley.

The Snake River splits into several channels around Oxbow Bend.

Mount Moran, little cousin of Grand Teton, nevertheless towers 6,000 ft. above Jackson Lake.

A vital step in the protection of the area was the addition of **Grand Teton National Park** to the south of Yellowstone beginning in the 1920s. Many dedicated people who have appreciated and loved the unspoiled beauty of the unique Snake River Valley known as Jackson Hole have united to preserve its pristine state. Despite strong pressures for commercialization and exploitation they have managed to maintain most of its integrity. John D. Rockefeller, Jr., recognizing the unique value of this treasure, added significantly to the size of the Park by donating private land.

The creation of Teton National Park and adjacent national forests has made possible the protection of the whole area around the town of Jackson and over 98% of the land in Teton County belongs to a government entity making what limited private land there is extremely valuable. The breathtaking vista of the Snake River Valley with the steep chain of the snow clad Teton Mountains rising to such a great height so sharply behind is unquestionably one of the world's most unforgettable and uplifting sights. There are countless trails for hikers and

many challenging ascents for mountain climbers to say nothing of the skiing possibilities.

Native Americans had been visiting the Jackson Hole area for countless millennia, but apparently it was unknown to Europeans until after 1800. What attracted the nomadic Indians was the abundant wildlife, especially the buffalo and elk, but they usually sought more temperate winter quarters as Jackson winters can be fierce. In the early 1800s trappers began to arrive in this productive hunting ground, mainly in search of beaver for which there was a great demand in Europe at the time. Many of these were French which is why so many of the place names around Jackson are in that language. The name of the Park itself comes from the French word for nipple of which the shape of the peaks reminded them.

Left page :
Canadian gray wolves introduced into Yellowstone Park have reproduced with surprising rapidity and now far surpass in numbers the original targets established. A rationale for wolf introduction was to thin elk herds in Yellowstone Park where there is no hunting, so that an over population was damaging riverine areas.
The wolves certainly controlled the Park's elk population, but there was nothing to stop them from spreading to an area many times the size of the Park itself where they were also protected, to the dismay of ranchers and hunters.

Next pages :
The work of erosion along the hills boarding the Gros Ventre river.

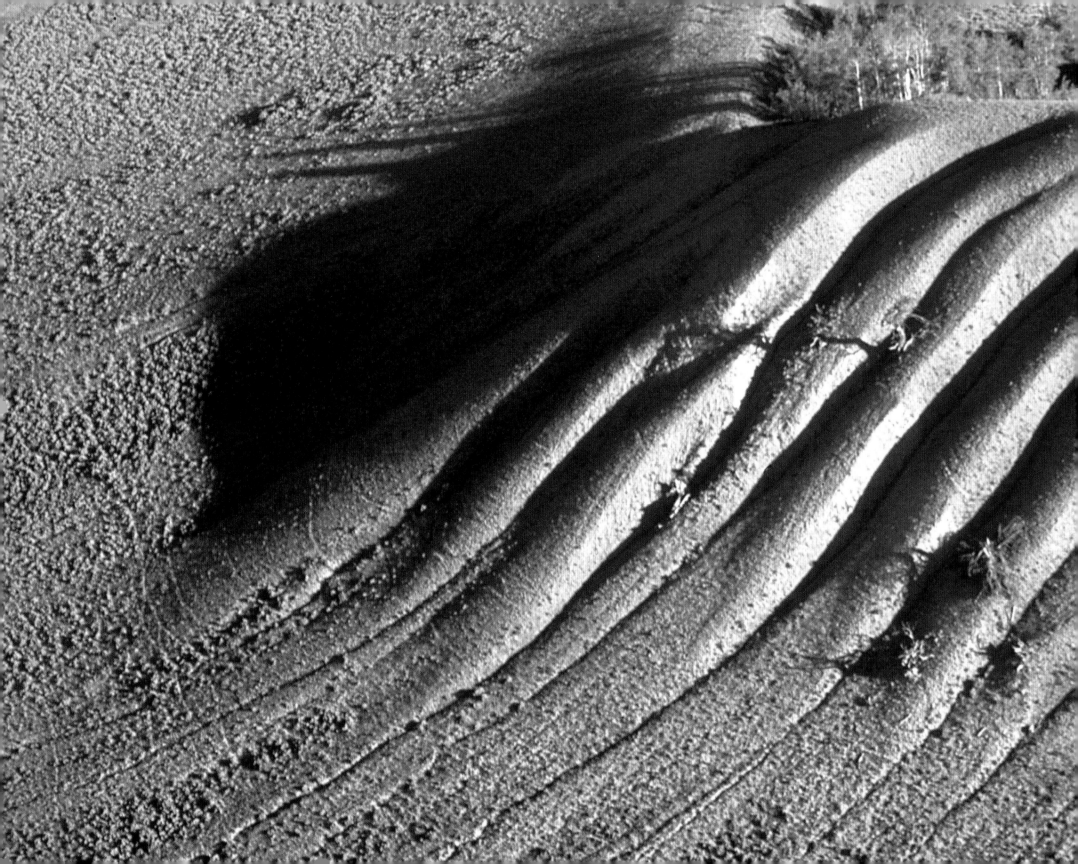

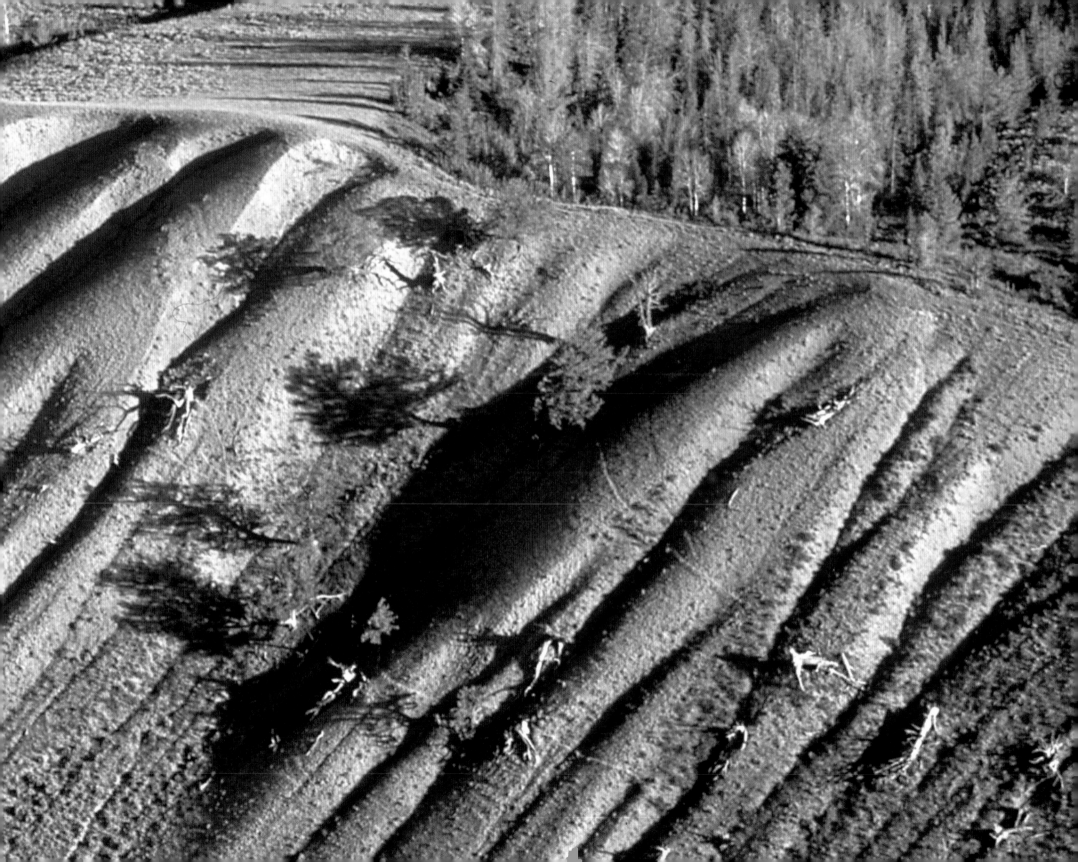

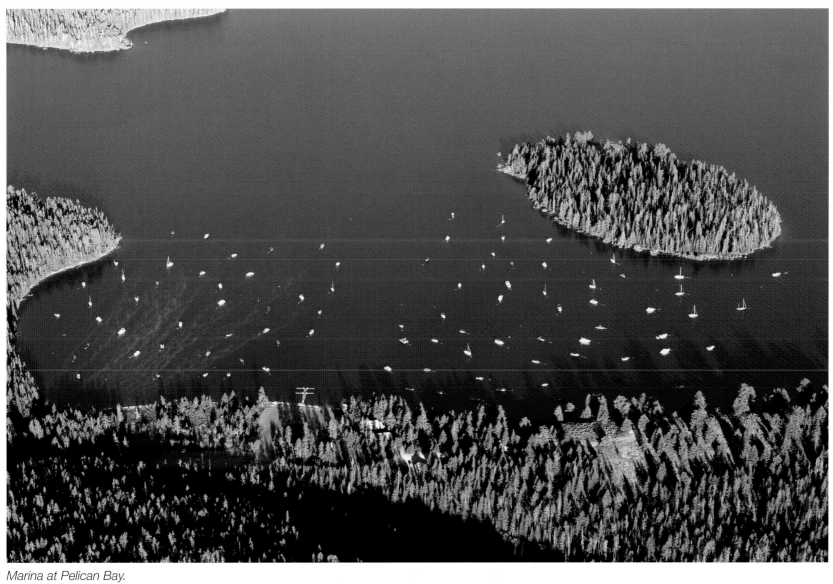

Marina at Pelican Bay.

THE WIND RIVER RANGE

The spectacular Wind River Range is the highest in Wyoming with 35 peaks over 13,000 ft., including Gannett Peak which even tops famous Grand Teton above Jackson Hole. No roads cross this hundred mile long chain of mountains which also form the Continental Divide. Most of it is Forest Service land and designated wilderness where no motors are allowed. A series of tumultuous volcanic and glacial forces have created over 2,000 lakes and ponds, many of which are stocked with trout including the prized golden trout. The Winds are also home to the nation's largest herd of bighorn sheep and provides habitat for elk, deer, moose, bear, wolves, wolverine and many other animals. The National Bighorn Sheep Center with excellent displays depicting these magnificent animals and their habitat is located in the little nearby town of Dubois. Before the arrival of domestic sheep, introduced by settlers, the wild bighorns were far more abundant. A tribe of Native Americans called the Sheepeaters or Tukudeka found an

Gannett Peak, Wyoming's highest mountain, is on the right.

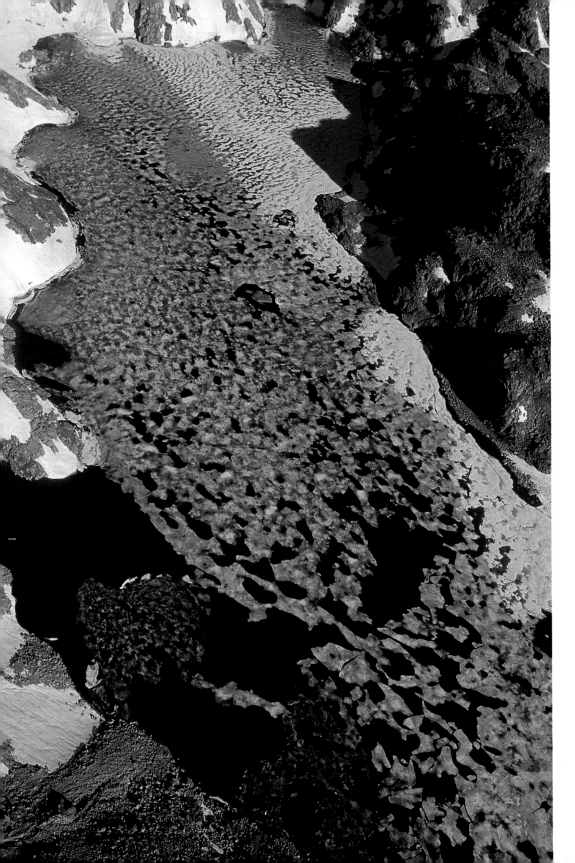

unusual niche for survival by hunting the wild sheep in the high mountains which they frequented even in winter when they fed on windswept slopes and lichen growing on rocks. This meant that the Sheepeaters also had to live high in Wyoming's rugged mountains near their source of food, but they adapted well to these difficult conditions and found comfortable shelters in remote Alpine valleys. They often hunted the sheep by driving them into funnel-like traps they built and killing them with the help of their powerful bows and fierce wolf-like dogs.

The Wind River Mountains are some of the most ancient in the world and are very different from the much newer Absarokas across the valley to the north. The Winds are crazily broken up terrain with sheer rock faces, deep gorges and all manner of unexpected outcroppings. Hard granite raised high long ago from far beneath the earth's crust predominates. The softer sedimentary material which used to be on top was eroded away or scraped off by the titanic power of immense gla-

Ice is still melting in July on this little lake.

ciers, sometimes 1,000 ft. thick, creeping slowly and inexorably, leaving the hard rock exposed. The glacial activity continued for many years and is still going on. The ice is now receding as global warming increases and how much of this is man-caused is a matter of fierce debate, but over the last million years there have been in the order of ten important swings of climate change when the glaciers expanded and receded. A few degrees can make all the difference. It has been a little over 10,000 years since the earth moved into its present warm cycle. The result of all this grinding back and forth in the Winds is to make them ideal for mountaineering because climbers can trust that their pitons will stick firmly and the rock will not split away at a crucial moment as it might in the Absarokas.

Wind River Country contributes to the world a different kind of product from oil or beef. The National Outdoor Leadership School, with its headquarters in the remote little town of Lander located at the base of the mountains, has touched many lives,

Next pages :
In the heart of the range : the circle of Towers.

not only in the US, but internationally. The school has over 120,000 graduates since it was begun in 1965 by that almost superhuman mountaineer, Paul Petzoldt. The challenging courses lasting up to three months teach survival, self-reliance, resourcefulness and leadership in a wilderness setting. The school is now running programs in many parts of the world, but its headquarters remain in Lander where it has 350 instructors based and an office staff of 140. It would be difficult to find a more appropriate setting for the operation than the vast, remote Wind River Mountains which tower above the town. The jagged mountains present all kinds of opportunities for mountaineering exercises, which are part of some of the NOLS training courses.

NOLS of course has no monopoly on the Winds and many mountaineers, hikers, fishermen and hunters have visited, loved and sometimes written about them. One of their attractions is that visiting them in any depth requires considerable physical effort. Thus they are still comparatively uncrowded

and visitors usually see few other people in contrast to places like Yellowstone Park.

One of the great sagas of the exploration of the West began on the Green River which rises on the south side of the Wind River Range and is one of the main tributaries of the Colorado. In 1869 John Wesley Powell's expedition was the first to make the perilous thousand mile descent of the Green and on down the Colorado and through the Grand Canyon, opening up the last large, unexplored tract of land in the Continental United States.

It was not only an amazing feat of courage, skill and determination, but it produced a wealth of useful scientific information about this hitherto unknown area.

Willow Lake and the Wind River Range seen from the Pinedale side.

43

From the Wind River Range, the Green River starts the trip to the Colorado River.

Left page :
The Blue Holes nestle in the foothills of the Wind River Range.

In the upper Green River, fall comes early in the mountains and groves of aspen, cottonwood and willow turn gold, yellow and orange as the elk begin to bugle for mates in the rutting season.
In the background, Green river lake and Squaretop mountain.

The Wind River Range is one of the oldest in the world. Its solid granite cliffs and glaciers present a glorious challenge for expert climbing enthusiasts. The many peaks on its remote hundred mile length have the added advantage of being uncrowded by other visitors.

Climbers who have reached the summit of Gannett Peak at 13,804 ft.

A herd of elk or wapiti on the side of Whiskey Mountain above Dubois.

OREGON TRAIL

By far the most important commercial activity in North America for several centuries was the fur trade. The first company of any kind to be established was the Hudson's Bay Company in 1670 and it remained the biggest and most powerful for many years, often filling the role of government in remote areas. French trappers from Quebec were the first Europeans to venture as far west as Wyoming. Sixty years before Lewis and Clark the French explorer, Pierre Gautier de la Verendrye, reached Wyoming and wrote a description of his journey for the French Government. It is partly from his account that we know the Indians here were just starting to acquire horses in the 1740s. French trappers must have been here well before that, but they left no written accounts.

At the dawn of the 19th century passage to the Pacific across the Rocky Mountains, especially one which could be traversed with wagons was not the obvious route it seems today. Jefferson made one of the great bargains of all time in 1803 with the Louisiana Purchase from a Napoleon blockaded on the European Continent by the British Navy.

South Pass provided the lowest and easiest path across the spine of the Continental Divide for wagon trains heading west

We gained almost a million square miles for $15 million or about 3 cents an acre. A large part of Wyoming was included. The time was ripe for the fledgling US to find out what it had really purchased and to begin its development. The first step was to send Lewis and Clark on their fabled 1804 journey to the Pacific which went up the Missouri River and crossed the Rockies by a very difficult route to reach the Pacific.

Certainly that expedition, which crossed to the north of Wyoming, provided a wealth of information, but it did not reveal a practical route for settlers to cross the Rockies. Distractions like the war of 1812 with Great Britain slowed a westward push, but meanwhile American mountain men like John Colter and Jim Bridger began to move into the Rockies in search of furs and adventure. This was the era of the legendary mountain man rendezvous, several of which were held in Wyoming, when they would come from hundreds of miles away to sell their pelts and buy the supplies they would need for another year. The most important prize was the beaver used for hats very much in vogue until the end of the 1830s when the style began to shift to silk. At the same time the beaver was nearly trapped out and the mountain men had to turn elsewhere for a living. Fortunately for some of them, settlers were just beginning to make the journey to the West Coast where there

were huge tracts of land with fertile soil and a temperate climate ideal for settlement to be had almost for the asking. The problem was getting there. The journey by ship was long, expensive and dangerous, often taking many months.

The most popular route was to cross the Rockies and the mountains beyond by wagon train on what became known as the Oregon Trail. They needed guides for the journey and the best qualified were the mountain men who knew the country and spoke the Indian languages. There was no easy way through and there was always the danger of attack from hostile and angry mounted warriors who had a deserved reputation of being the best light cavalry in the world. In reality Indian attacks on this route were rare and the tribesmen these pioneers encountered were more often inclined to trade peacefully. A far greater danger was disease and thousands died of cholera which took the lives of over half of some groups. The journey was 2,000 miles and they needed to get over the mountain passes before the heavy snows set in or they could perish on the way; not easy to accomplish when 15 miles a day was making good time.

The best route for wagon trains via Wyoming's South Pass was discovered by accident in 1811 by Robert Stuart who was working for John Jacob Astor's Pacific Fur Trading

Coampany in an unsuccessful attempt to establish a head-quarters at the mouth of the Columbia. The Indians had been using the route for centuries, but it was previously unknown to Europeans. Later the Union Pacific and US route I-80 follow part of the same path through this gateway in the Rockies. Between 1836 and 1869 about a half a million people made the journey. The ruts left by so many wagons are still visible today. The California Gold Rush of 1849 gave a huge impulse to the traffic which continued until the completion of the transcontinental railway in 1868. The railway opened ridiculously easy access compared to the laborious progress of the ox cart, but the earlier influx of Oregon Trail arrivals enabled the United States to secure California, Oregon and Washington from Mexico and Great Britain who also had territorial claims to the area.

The famous Mormon Trail which led to the settlement of Utah followed the same route through South Pass, but diverged farther on to head toward Salt Lake instead of continuing farther west. The Mormons had been persecuted in their original homes in the Mid West on account of their unorthodox religious beliefs and their leader, Joseph Smith, had been killed. They therefore sought an unpopulated area where they could avoid persecution and Utah as no one else had

The famous landmark of Split Rock rises behind an irrigated hay field.

yet settled there. In 1847 when they first arrived, this territory was not even officially part of the Untied States though Mexico ceded it to us the following year. The Mormons continued to travel to Utah by this trail for another 20 years with almost incredible determination facing horrendous privations and hardships. When they had not the means to buy wagons and oxen they used hand carts and sometimes perished along the way when they failed to cross the mountains of Wyoming before the snow came.

The fabulous feats of the Pony Express riders make one of the most notable and romantic stories of the Oregon Trail. For a year and a half around the time of the outbreak of the Civil War they provided a much faster and critical communications link which greatly facilitated business transactions and helped solidify California's adherence to the Union cause. The fact that they were able to cover the 2,000 miles from St. Joseph, Missouri to Sacramento in 7 to 10 days, often through hostile Indian country, is a tribute to the courage and skill of the riders and to the careful planning of the organizers who had to set up relay stations every ten miles or so along the way. "Buffalo Bill" Cody was the most famous of these riders and the superb Buffalo Bill Historical Center in Cody bears his name. It became redundant later in 1861 with the completion of the transcontinental telegraph line, but it will remain a shining symbol of Western history and enterprise.

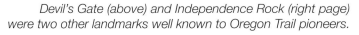

Devil's Gate (above) and Independence Rock (right page) were two other landmarks well known to Oregon Trail pioneers.

THE RED DESERT

Wyoming's Red Desert is little known, but it is one of the most fascinating parts of the state and though the area is larger than New Jersey it has almost no human habitation. Very low rainfall and scarce water supplies make most of it impossible for agriculture except for a few places which can be irrigated. It lies directly on the Continental Divide and surrounds the unusual pocket known as the Great Divide which is a basin of 4,000 square miles from which no streams flow out in any direction. If there were heavier rain or snowfall, it would become a huge lake, but precipitation is so sparse that it evaporates or soaks into the ground before large quantities can accumulate. A few small lakes and ponds are left by melting snow. There are some year around water courses like Muddy Creek outside the Great Divide basin which provide habitat for some very rare fish and reptiles. The old trails headed west like the Oregon Trail passed this way until the transcontinental railway was completed in 1868. Now the railway line and route I-80 pass through the southern end of the Desert.

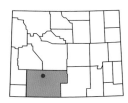

The Killpecker Dunes are one of the world's largest active sand dune areas.

Two bikers race across the sand dunes of the Red Desert.

The Boar's Tusk in the Great Divide Basin was another famous landmark for Oregon Trail travelers.

The colorful topography is similar to Monument Valley in many ways. Volcanoes, glaciers and erosion have left an array of bizarre formations. Shifting red sand dunes blown about by the wind are the largest in the United States and provide reservoirs to store the scarce moisture helping to provide habitat for animals like white footed mice, pygmy rabbits and kangaroo rats. The huge expanse of the Red Desert makes it a refuge for other animals like pronghorn antelope, desert elk, mule deer, mountain lions, bob cats. There is also considerable variety of bird life including trumpeter swans, white pelicans, golden eagles, and many kinds of hawks and owls.

Best known of all the animals on the Red Desert is the wild mustang where over a thousand of them now have their home. In the 19th century herds of mustangs, thought to have numbered over 3 million, roamed the open plains from Texas to Montana. Apparently the horse originated in North America and some of them migrated across the Bering Straits during the Ice Age to gain a strong foothold in Asia.

Next page :
a large herd of wild mustangs galloping on Antelope Hills.

60

They became extinct in America about 10,000 years ago, possibly due to over hunting by Native Americans. At any rate, for millennia there were no horses here until the Spanish invasion and in the 16th century the Conquistadores brought thousands of horses over from Spain. Of course the horse gave them an enormous military advantage and they guarded them jealously from the native people quite successfully until their expansion suffered a sharp reversal during the Pueblo Revolt of 1680 in New Mexico when a thousand or more horses escaped or fell into Indian hands. This this provided considerable stock for wild herds and for the use of Indian tribes like the Comanche and Apache who began trading them with tribes farther north.

The habitat was ideal for horses which have little difficulty in adjusting quickly to a feral state since they are large, powerful, swift, alert and intelligent. Then as now, predators like mountain lions and wolves managed to kill them only rarely. With an excellent food supply they multiplied rapidly and by the 1730s began to arrive in large numbers in Wyoming where local tribes were acquiring them either by trade or by catching and taming wild ones. Many of these horses came from Barb and Arabian stock brought to Spain by Moorish invaders and had excellent bloodlines. Plains Indian tribes like the Shoshone, the Crow and the Arapahoe quickly grasped the tremendous advantages offered them by horses. The buffalo dominated the Great Plains in their tens of millions and supplied the natives with food, clothing, tools, lodging and often fuel for their fires, but hunting these large animals, which could easily outdistance a man on foot, was difficult indeed and they often resorted to tactics like stampeding a herd over a cliff. Another strategy was to put on a wolf pelt and try to crawl up within bowshot. Packs of wolves constantly followed the buffalo waiting for a chance to pick off the old or the sick and they caused little

alarm. Now suddenly a mounted warrior could go faster than a buffalo and drive arrows or lances into them at the run. Horses also enabled the Indians to move camp faster and with more equipment to follow the migrating buffalo herds which were often on the move in search of better grazing. The advent of the horse amounted to a technological empowerment which vastly improved their economic base and transformed their society almost overnight. Within a generation they became some of the best horsemen the world has ever known and it made them far more dangerous enemies when they were on the warpath either against other tribes or white intruders. The glory days of the mounted Indian lasted perhaps a century and half, but they were finished by the 1880s with the extermination of the buffalo and the influx of white settlers. Thus the Indian horse culture went from a sudden climb to affluence and power to degrading defeat in a comparatively short time.

Wild horses, like the mounted Indians and the buffalo lost most of their free ranging habitat. Many were captured and tamed to make wonderful mounts for cowboys, ranchers and Pony Express riders. Still many protected wild horse herds do remain in Wyoming thanks in part to the Federal Government. In 1971, the United States Congress recognized Mustangs as «living symbols of the historic and pioneer spirit of the West, which continue to contribute to the diversity of life forms within the Nation and enrich the lives of the American people.» Those of us who love horses and riding are gratified by this tribute. Thus there are now over a dozen places scattered over the state where there are wild horses. The Pryor Mountain herd is noteworthy for having mainly Spanish stock, indicating that they are descended from the original wild mustangs and the horses there are probably the easiest to observe. The Red Desert herd is the largest, but it is spread out over a vast area and the horses are not always easy to find. The wild horses personify a spirit of freedom, resourcefulness and courage surviving in the face of great odds.

The Great Divide Basin where water flows out neither to the east nor to the west with the Oregon Buttes in the background.

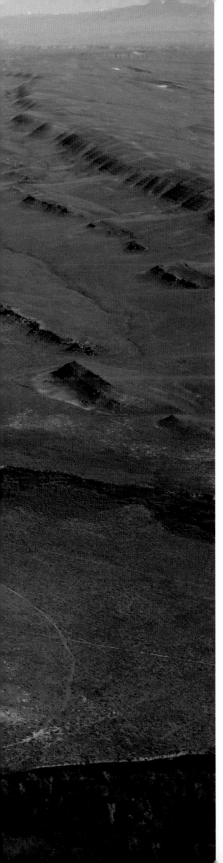

THE WIND RIVER INDIAN RESERVATION

Wyoming has one of the largest Indian reservations in the US called the Wind River Reservation which covers an area half the size of New Jersey. It extends over a large part of the Wind River Valley and the surrounding mountains with good farm land and excellent hunting and fishing. It has significant oil and natural gas production which provide royalties to the tribes and it is inherently one of the most desirable of all the country's reservations. The land was originally given to the Shoshone Tribe on the comparatively early date of 1868 because, under the wise leadership of Chief Washakie, they had been indispensable allies of the US cavalry against their ancient enemies like the Sioux and other tribes hostile to white encroachment. Washakie was a towering figure of exceptional stature who dominated the history of the Wind River Valley for most of the 19th century. He lived to be a hundred years old and led his people through a time of enormous change. Washakie understood that winning an occasional battle and plundering a few wagon trains would not stem the flood of immigrants. The pyrrhic victory of the Sioux at the Battle of the Little Big Horn led only to far more trouble for them. His foresight, integrity and magnanimity shine at a time of violence, greed and bitter rivalry.

Initially Washakie won leadership of the Shoshone through his outstanding prowess as a warrior and military strategist in battling surrounding hostile tribes like the Sioux, Crow, Cheyenne and Arapahoe. The best known of his many exploits was at the Battle of Crowheart Butte. The butte itself is an impressive landmark which thrusts up dramatically from the floor of the Wind River Valley near the center of what is now Fremont County.

Wiew of the reservation with the Little Wind River.

Rattlesnake ridge.

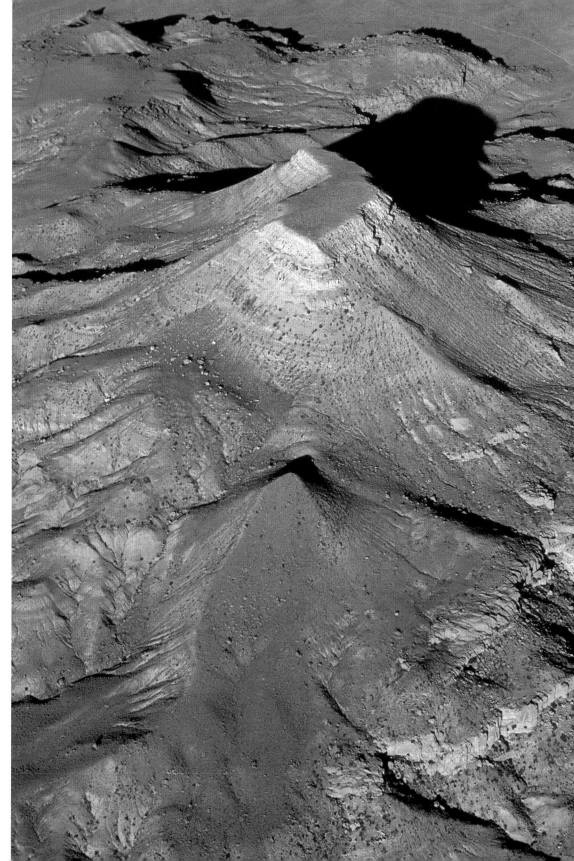

The Plains Indian tribes had always struggled with one another for hunting rights and the acquisition of the horse made these conflicts more acute and frequent. There are varying contradictory accounts of the battle, but perhaps this version is as good as any. The Crows under their chief, Big Robber, tried a test of strength and began hunting near Crowheart Butte, not far from where Washakie and his tribe of Shoshones had an encampment. The fighting which ensued caused grievous casualties on both sides, so they decided to settle the dispute by a hand to hand fight between the two chiefs.

They rode out like knights of old with their lances and their shields to fight to the death. Washakie triumphed and either as a sign of respect or in victory celebration he cut out the heart of the Crow chief.

Some accounts say that he placed the heart on the tip of his lance; others that he ate it. Whatever the truth may be, the name persists.

A decade after the Shoshone had settled on the Reservation an agreement was reached to allow

Crowheart Butte.

several thousand Indians from the Northern Arapahoe Tribe to settle there also and they moved mainly into the eastern end while the Shoshone stayed on the western side. The two tribes were traditional enemies with many important cultural differences and some frictions remain, but they have managed to live together peacefully now for over a century.

A colorful cultural life flourishes today on the Reservation, adding greatly to the allure of Wind River Country for the visitor. Several Powwows are held each year where Indian dancers perform in magnificent traditional costumes complete with eagle feather headdresses and

beaded leather clothing. The dances represent themes like hunting, tracking and war while there is chanting and incessant drum beating. The dancers often imitate the movements of animals. The buffalo has particular importance because it provided much of the food, tools and clothing for the Plains Indians. Dance groups from the Reservation perform frequently.

The sacred Sundance ceremony takes place around the summer solstice each year, is an integral part of the pre-Columbian Indian religion and is taken very seriously. Outsiders can observe, but no pictures are allowed. The ceremony lasts up to a week and includes dancing, drumming, visions and fasting. The ancient religion had many aspects of pantheism and showed great respect for animals as spiritual beings. It had much in common with the teachings of Saint Francis of Assisi. The ceremony is an affirmation of the necessity for harmony between all living things and a celebration of rebirth and renewal. Recently several successful casinos have been started on the Reservation which help provide income for education and health care as well as employment for local people.

Fort Washakie is the main city and administrative capital (left page).
Crow Creek curve between the red hills on the north of the reservation (above).

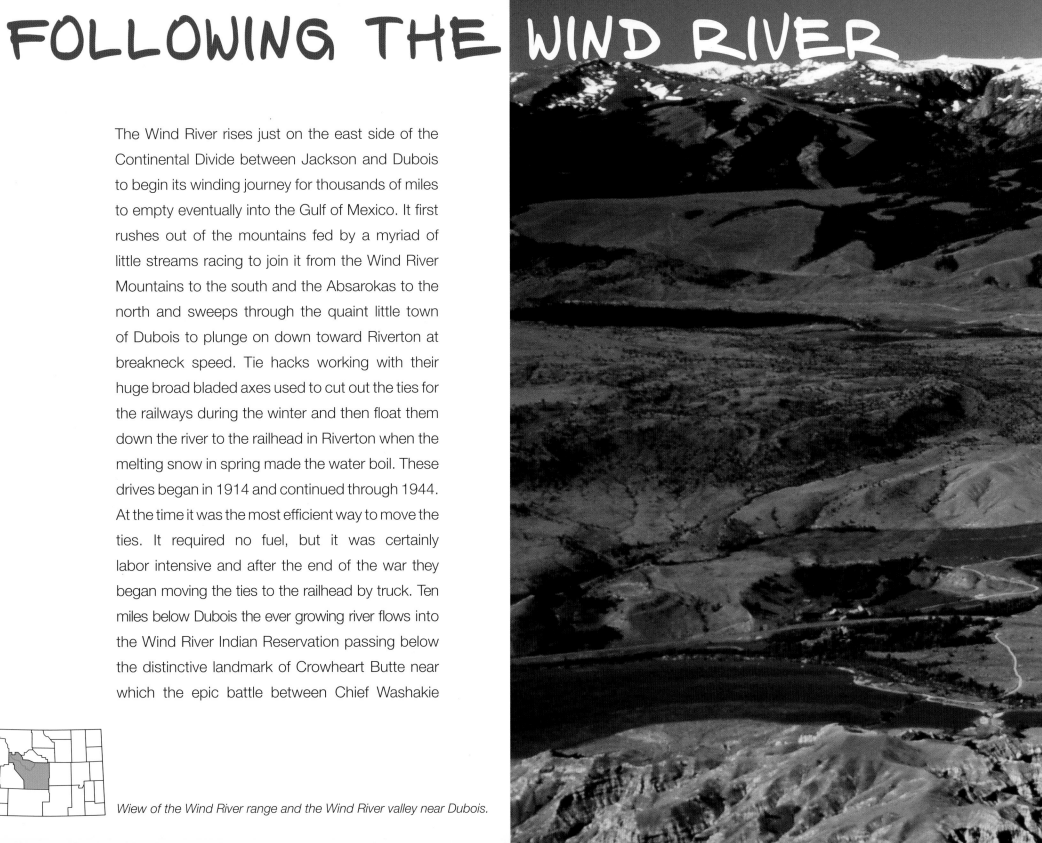

FOLLOWING THE WIND RIVER

The Wind River rises just on the east side of the Continental Divide between Jackson and Dubois to begin its winding journey for thousands of miles to empty eventually into the Gulf of Mexico. It first rushes out of the mountains fed by a myriad of little streams racing to join it from the Wind River Mountains to the south and the Absarokas to the north and sweeps through the quaint little town of Dubois to plunge on down toward Riverton at breakneck speed. Tie hacks working with their huge broad bladed axes used to cut out the ties for the railways during the winter and then float them down the river to the railhead in Riverton when the melting snow in spring made the water boil. These drives began in 1914 and continued through 1944. At the time it was the most efficient way to move the ties. It required no fuel, but it was certainly labor intensive and after the end of the war they began moving the ties to the railhead by truck. Ten miles below Dubois the ever growing river flows into the Wind River Indian Reservation passing below the distinctive landmark of Crowheart Butte near which the epic battle between Chief Washakie

Wiew of the Wind River range and the Wind River valley near Dubois.

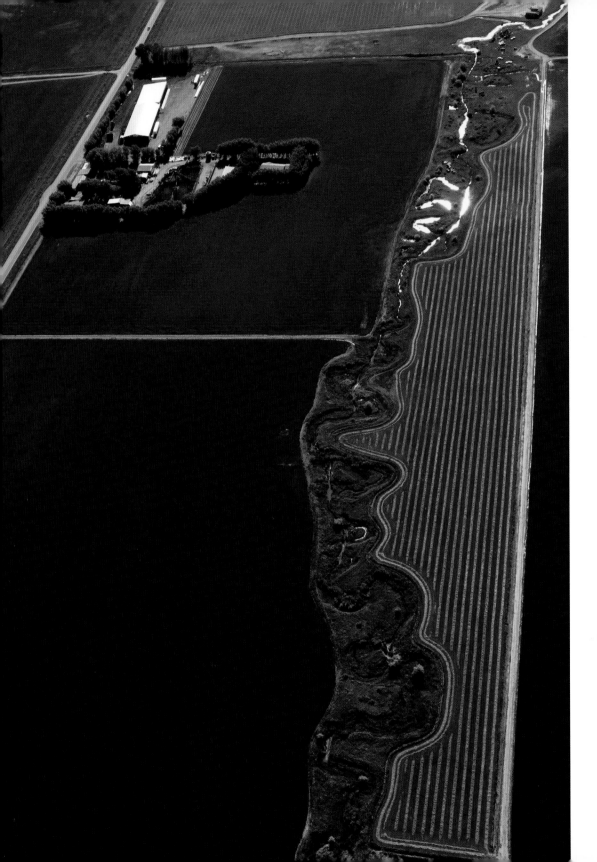

of the Shoshone and Chief Big Robber of the Crows took place in 1866. A little farther down, the River is joined by an important tributary called Bull Creek where a dam has been built creating an 8 mile long reservoir which catches water from the spring snow melt and releases it more gradually through the summer as the flow in the main Wind River diminishes. This makes it possible to irrigate many acres below and to still keep a good flow in the Wind River which holds some fine trout.

After passing through Riverton the river makes a sharp turn north and heads for the Wind River Canyon where it has cut a narrow passage 2,500 ft. deep through the Owl Creek Mountains exposing a few billion years of geological activity to view. The stretch of highway running through the canyon between Shoshoni and Thermopolis richly deserves its designation as a scenic highway. A dam has been built at the entrance to the canyon which backs the river up for 20 miles behind offering a large lake with excellent fishing and boating possibilities. At the bottom end of the Wind River Canyon the name is abruptly changed with

Irrigation water from the Wind River makes rich fields productive in contrast to the neighboring arid badlands.

Crowheart butte.

A herd of wild horses running free near Black Mountain and Crow Creek on the Wind River Indian Reservation.

little obvious excuse to the Big Horn River. The reason for the name change seems to be that until a road and railway was finally put through the Canyon a little more than a hundred years ago there was no passage possible for travelers so that a long detour was needed for people crossing the Owl Creek Mountains. Apparently when the rivers were named people on each side did not make the connection.

After the Canyon the River flows on north past the town of Thermopolis which claims the world's largest hot springs. These are open to the public and are a popular bathing place. Well preserved dinosaur remains have been found nearby which attract many visitors. The river continues north through fertile valleys which it irrigates until it reaches the Yellowtail Reservoir just across the border in Montana and forms another artificial lake far south into Wyoming which also has excellent recreational value.

The Wind River Canyon between Boysen Reservoir and Thermopolis.

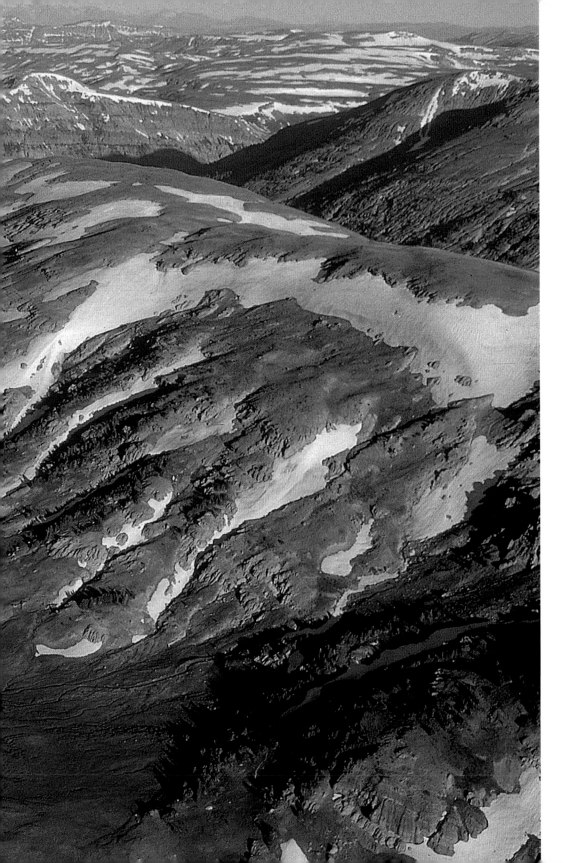

ABSAROKA MOUNTAINS

The Absaroka Mountain Range in northwest Wyoming covers a vast stretch of wild, unspoiled country 150 miles long and 75 miles wide. The Range extends into Yellowstone Park and the edge of southern Montana. It forms part of the Greater Yellowstone Ecosystem, the largest wild ecosystem left in the lower 48 states. Much of the area is administered by the Shoshone National Forest, the first national forest in the US.

A striking feature of the Absarokas is its vast Alpine meadows interspersed with forests of pine, spruce and aspen. The meadows provide rich and abundant feed for a broad array of wildlife as the melting snow leaves the ground moist and fertile. This is the time with a myriad of wildflowers of almost countless varieties begin to appear and cover the slopes with a wide display of changing colors. In late June many meadows and hillsides turn a glorious pink with a profusion of bitterroot flowers. These plants have an unusually large root which provided an important part of the diet for

Late july over the Absaroka mountains.

The Dunoir River above Dubois twists and turns through the valley like a huge blue snake.

Behind Brooks Lake the steep cliffs of the Pinnacle Buttes rise sharply to form the Continental Divide.

Pilot peak like a sentinel near the Montana border.

Cliffs and peaks in the North Absaroka Wilderness.

the local Indian tribes like the Shoshone, Sioux, Blackfoot and Crow. The women worked hard to harvest as many as they could with their digging sticks before they began to bloom and become bitter. The gaudy yellow of balsam arrowleaf covers many slopes at about the same time. The pale blue, sweet smelling lupine also begins to bloom early and keeps doing so until the very end of summer. Aside from game meat one of the most important sources of protein for the Indians in this area was the white bark pine nut. These trees are closely related to the limber pine, but grow at higher altitudes just below the tree line. They are one of the most important foods for grizzly bears. It is worrying that of late years a particularly virulent pine bark beetle infestation is killing many of them, seriously impacting the diet of these omnivorous bears which can digest anything from pine nuts and roots to ants and carrion.

The Sheep Eater Indians or Tukudeka, a branch of the Shoshone, carved out an unusual niche for themselves in the high Alpine regions of the Absarokas where they spent the whole year rather than

The Diamond D ranch along Horse creek.

The Washakie Needles and Dome Mountain near the southeastern end of the Absarokas.

migrating from mountain to valley as did most of the Indians and the wild animals. Like other tribes, they collected pine nuts and roots, but their main source of food was the bighorn sheep which were abundant in the area and which also stay high during the winter feeding on windswept slopes and lichen. The Absarokas offer outstanding recreational opportunities with many blue ribbon trout streams, excellent hunting for trophy animals, hiking and wilderness pack trips.

A herd of elk resting in the warmth of the sun.

Trees burned by forest fire.

Early morning frost on Two Oceans Peak.

THE BIGHORN MOUNTAINS

The Big Horn Mountains slash a 40 miles swath for nearly a hundred miles down from the Montana border into north central Wyoming, splitting the Great Plains and leaving the Big Horn Basin to the west and the Powder River Basin to the east. The Bighorn National Forest encompasses most of the area and includes over a million acres of land. The chain rises to over 13 000 ft. at the highest point and its higher elevations are only free of snow in July and August. Three scenic highways cross these mountains affording spectacular views of the surrounding country. They formed a difficult barrier for early settlers who had to pass either to the north or south of the range. The Big Horns provide excellent habitat for fish and wildlife with vast forests of spruce, aspen, fir and pine. Many lakes and streams with trout are hidden in remote places which must be reached by horseback or on foot.

In spring and summer a profusion of wildflowers bring glorious colors to the mountain meadows where elk and deer graze. Cattle feed for a short time in the summer in some lower parts of the mountains eating the coarser fodder and improving

Cloud Peak, rising to 13 167 feet.
is the highest point in the Bighorn Mountains.

The tall spine of the Bighorn Mountains was uplifted about 70 million years ago from what had been a huge lake rich in fossils. The sediment from this titanic event was deposited in the Bighorn Basin to the west and especially in the Powder River Basin to the east which helped create the rich fossil fuels being extracted there today.

the range for wildlife. A network of trails for hikers and horsemen is maintained in the high country offering many diverse opportunities. Fishermen can find remote, uncrowded spots for their sport and it is an excellent area for hunters in the fall. The Big Horns are also the unlikely seeming home for the Medicine Wheel, one of the most fascinating relics of pre-Columbian Native American construction in the United States probably dating back 500 to 800 years. It is still of great spiritual importance to nearby tribes though we know little about who actually built it or what ceremonies may have been conducted there. Inexplicably it is located high on a fairly flat, treeless area at nearly 10,000 ft. only accessible for a few months in the summer. The pattern of the wheel is formed by large rocks and consists of a round circle 80 ft. in diameter with 28 internal spokes and stone cairns stacked up in meaningful places. The number 28 represents the days of the lunar month, but an intriguing study by the Stanford Solar Center has found that the orientation of the spokes and cairns shows a surprisingly sophisticated knowledge of astrology.

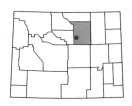

The remote Hole in the Wall area was used in the 1890's by Butch Cassidy's Wild Bunch and many other outlaws as a hideout.

The city of Buffalo.

The Bighorn National Forest on the east side of the mountains.

Canyon in the Shell area.

Over millions of years erosion has carved out deep canyons and washed away softer material to form strange designs in the topography of the foothills along the Bighorns.

Using information from many sources as well as their own investigations, the Solar Center has put together some interesting facts and theories. It was easy to figure out that two of the main spokes and cairns point to the place of the rising sun at summer solstice, but with deeper investigation less obvious and more sophisticated aspects of significance emerge like probable alignments with stars. The Big Horn Medicine Wheel has been designated a National Historic Landmark.

At the southern end of the Bighorns and in striking contrast to the significance of the Medicine Wheel lies another symbol of Wyoming's history of less shining repute. Though it has not achieved the status of a National Historic Landmark, it nevertheless holds a preeminent place in legends, films and books about the West. This is the remote Hole-in-the-Wall, ideal headquarters for many outlaw gangs from the 1860s into the early 20th century. It lies far from any towns in country cut up by steep gorges and rugged mountains. The name came from the fact that it is located just below the only passage on horseback for many

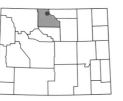

The Medecine Wheel.

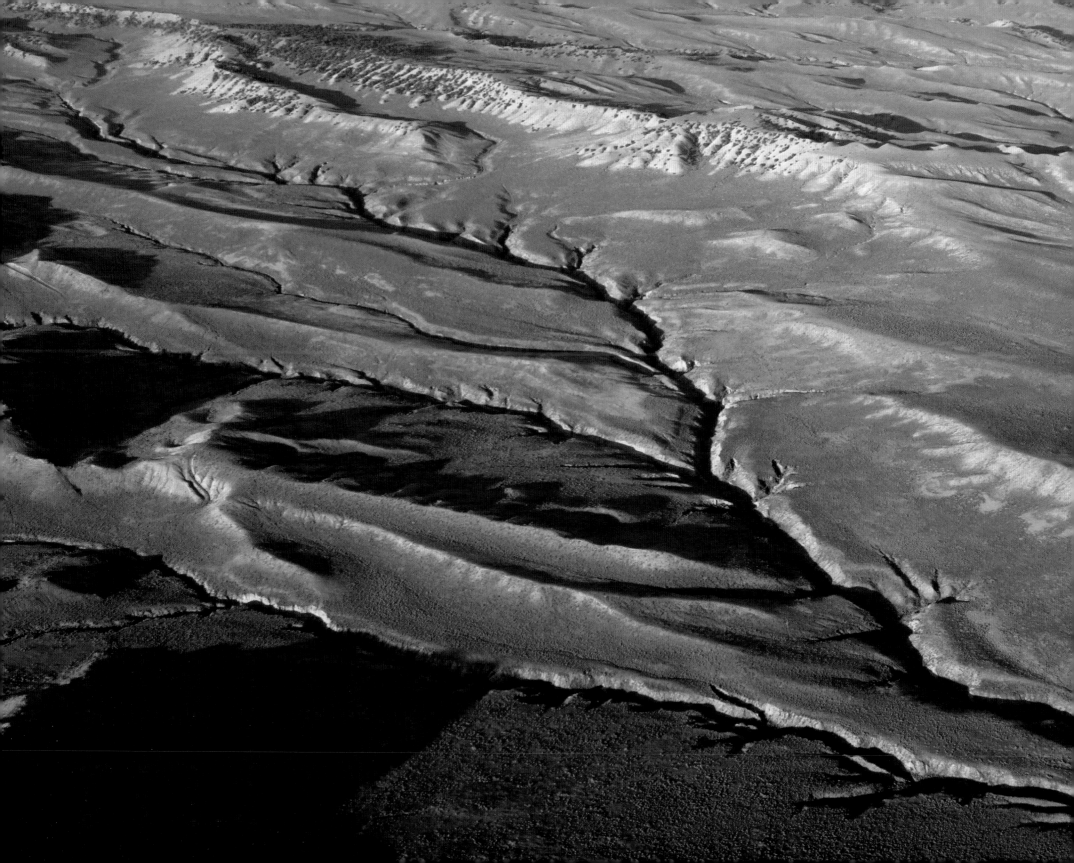

miles through what is called the "red wall", a 50 mile long spine of rock several hundred feet high. The outlaws could see anyone coming from miles away in any direction. There were good pastures nearby where rustlers could keep their stolen cattle while they looked for a market.

Outlaw gangs like Butch Cassidy's Wild Bunch had a whole series of hideouts all through Wyoming and into neighboring states. One of the most effective techniques in helping well organized gangs to evade pursuit after robbery of a bank, train or stagecoach was to have a string of fresh horses stashed at strategic points so that the tired horses of the posse would fall far behind and lose the trail.

Another place of extremely ill repute located to the southeast of the Hole-in-the-Wall in the Powder River Basin is the Teapot Dome. The rich oil reserves in this neighborhood were the root cause of the greatest scandal every to strike the political scene of the United States until Watergate. It demolished the reputations of some of the nation's most powerful people including that of President Harding, though he was dead by the time it came to light. He had allowed the Secretary of the Interior to put some of the nation's best oil reserves in the hands of rich oil men to do with as they liked and reap huge profits at public expense.

Chimney Rock at Shell.

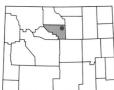

Ten Sleep at canyon's gate.

JACKSON HOLE, WINTER PARADISE

Undoubtedly Jackson Hole is one of the world's premier resorts for skiing and other winter sports. Its well connected airport (by far the most active in the state) makes it easily accessible with direct flights from many major cities. The ski runs have a rare vertical drop of over 4,000 ft. and it is blessed with an abundance of deep, light, powder snow, but the ideal conditions are not the only attraction. The breathtaking beauty of the Jackson Hole area is unique. The spectacular way that the Teton Mountain Range towers nearly 8,000 ft. almost straight up above the Snake River Valley provides an unsurpassed view. The line of perpetually snow clad peaks gleams above the wide, fertile valley where the river sometimes cascades in white water plumes and sometimes meanders in peaceful bends. Just up the valley from the town buffalo still roam and bald eagles swoop from the sky to seize native cutthroat trout from the river. The National Elk Refuge on the outskirts of town provides winter habitat for thousands of elk and it is easy to observe them nosing unconcernedly for forage through the snow.

The town of Jackson Hole, a pearl in the heart of the Rockies.

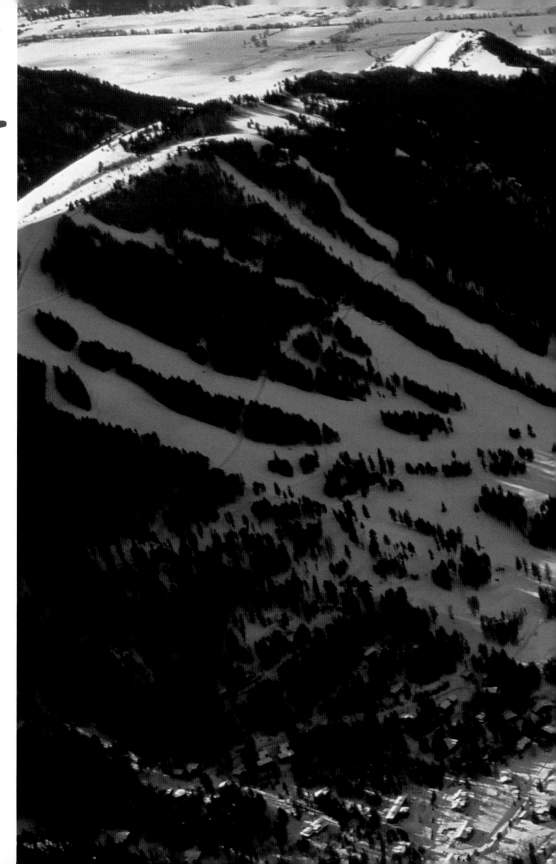

Teton Village is undoubtedly one of the world's premier ski resorts with superb downhill slopes of unusual length which challenge the most expert skiers. It has many luxury hotels and fine restaurants for dining. The nearby town of Jackson has many attractions for shopping, sightseeing and nightlife.

While Jackson has some of the most challenging slopes in the world which attract top skiers internationally, it also has intermediate slopes and excellent places for beginners as well. The list of winter sports around Jackson doesn't stop with downhill skiing as it also excellent for snowboarding, cross

A herd of elk feeding on the National Elk Reserve.

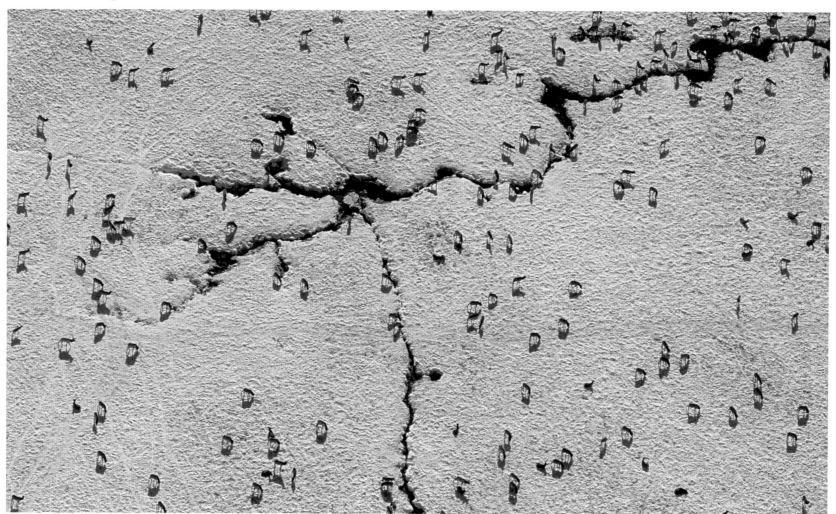

country skiing, snowmobiling, snowshoeing, dog sledding and snow coach touring. A popular excursion is riding in a horse drawn sleigh through the 25,000 acre National Elk Refuge where over 7,000 elk pass the winter. It is the largest elk herd in the world. They are fed here now in the winter since the town of Jackson has taken much of their traditional winter habitat and disturbed their migration routes farther south.

Because of the unique advantages provided by nature, the small town of Jackson (about 12,000 inhabitants) has attracted many talented people giving it an unusually rich and vibrant cultural life. Many art galleries offer a stunning array of photographs and paintings. The exquisite National Museum of Wildlife Art overlooking the National Elk Refuge contains some of the world's artistic masterpieces relating to wildlife. There is a broad choice of restaurants catering to a wide range of palettes. Some top chefs have been drawn here because the life style appeals to them. For those who have the energy after a day of sport, there are also some lively night clubs.

TAMING THE RIVERS

Many of the nation's great rivers both on the east and the west side of the Continental Divide have their source in Wyoming's mountains. These rivers are of vital importance to Wyoming and the states they traverse below as they open up huge tracts of land for agriculture and allow generation of large amounts of clean hydroelectric power as well as providing marvelous opportunities for recreation. Most of the land drained by these rivers requires irrigation to produce agricultural crops effectively. Today the average American is almost totally detached from agriculture, but it is still our largest export at about $100 billion a year and goes a long way to making up for the deficit in foreign trade caused by oil imports. With our own numbers growing rapidly and the world population increasing by nearly 100 million a year, our food supply is likely to have an ever growing importance. We are on a collision course as growing cities gobble up more agricultural land and water now used for irrigation, while at the same time requiring more food for a larger population.

Flaming Gorge Reservoir.

John Wesley Powell gave this section of the Green River its appropriate name as he made his epic journey down the Green into the Colorado and through the Grand Canyon. There is now a dam and reservoir which helps to control the unruly waters of the river. The lake created is a popular recreation area with excellent fishing and many inlets to explore by boat.

Wyoming's rivers rise in the mountains and their flow has disrupting spikes caused by the melting snow in the spring and much lower flows in late summer, fall and winter. This poses great problems for hydroelectric power generation and for irrigation if the water cannot be stored in reservoirs and released gradually. In some years especially, the spring runoff causes disastrous floods downstream which can be mitigated by keeping some of it behind dams in reservoirs.

On the west side of the Continental Divide the most important rivers are the Snake and the Green. The Snake River rises in Yellowstone Park and flows south through Jackson Hole before turning west into Idaho and joining the Columbia. One dam on the Snake in Wyoming raises the level of

Jackson Lake by 30 ft. and stores water for later use below. The Green River flows south out of the Wind River Mountains to the Colorado River along the route of John Wesley Powell's ground-breaking descent to discover a whole new part of the southwest including the Grand Canyon. These days only a trickle of water from the Colorado River reaches the Pacific Ocean after making possible many irrigation systems and supplying cities along the way.

On the east side of the Divide the Wind River has a long journey to the Gulf of Mexico. After traversing the Wind River valley it turns sharply north and becomes the Big Horn which eventually empties into the Missouri and the Mississippi. Twenty mile long Boysen Reservoir at the head of the Wind River Canyon makes possible the generation of electric power and the irrigation of fertile land below. The North Platte River begins in Colorado, but then flows north for hundreds of miles through Wyoming before crossing into Nebraska. The Oregon Trail route used to follow the North Platte up from Nebraska as far as Casper where it branched off to head for South Pass and the Great Divide. Now several important dams on the North Platte form large reservoirs which provide excellent fishing and boating opportunities and are popular with tourists as well as Wyoming residents.

The waters of Yellowtail Reservoir reach fingers far up the canyons along the shore.

120

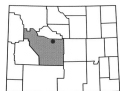

Boysen Reservoir.

Glendo Reservoir.

MEDECINE BOW MOUNTAINS

The Medicine Bow Mountains in southeastern Wyoming stretch for 150 miles from Colorado up into central Wyoming and are a popular place for hiking, mountain climbing, fishing and hunting. The unusual name derives from the customs of the Indian tribes which used to visit the area like the Arapahoe, Sioux and Shoshone. A kind of tree growing there known as the mountain mahogany was favored by the Indians for making bows. It is a very dense wood which will sink in water while still green and is ideal for making a powerful bow. The Indians used to come frequently to cut these trees for that purpose. At the same time the tribes used to seek medicinal plants growing in the same general area and it was often a time of peaceful intertribal relations.

The mountains provide good habitat for many animals like mule deer, moose, elk, bear, bighorn sheep, lynx, bobcat and many smaller animals. Beaver make their dams in some of the streams and there is a wide variety of birds. In summer cattle graze in some parts of the national forest.

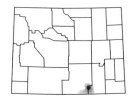

Many lakes reflect on Snowy Range Pass.

Lake Marie and the Snowy Range.

FOLLOWING PLATTE RIVER

Though it rises in Colorado, the North Platte is one of Wyoming's great rivers and it runs through several hundred miles of the State before crossing into Nebraska. Before the transcontinental railway was completed the wagon trains headed westward followed the North Platte from its confluence with the Missouri as far as Casper where it branched off toward the Sweetwater River and South Pass. The wagon trains had to have water and feed for their oxen and horses so they needed to stay as close as possible to a supply of both, which the Platte afforded.

The Oregon Trail and other trails like the California Trail and the Mormon Trail followed much the same route through Wyoming and usually it was more of a corridor than a single path. Fort Laramie on the banks of the North Platte where wagon trains often crossed the river was the first major stop on the Trail in Wyoming.

Several trails which had followed different routes met there to reach a comparatively narrow corridor on the 250 mile stretch from Fort Laramie. The town which became Fort Laramie was first set up as a fur trading post and did not become a military fort until 1849 in order to protect travelers from Indian attack.

The flow of travelers headed on up the Platte gave a number of little towns in Wyoming their start as stores and blacksmith shops were set up to service the wagon trains. From time to time the River had to be crossed and this could be a difficult problem as emigrants had to begin quite early in the spring in order to get over the mountains by the time the first snows were starting. This meant that they were obliged to cross the rivers when they were high with melting snow. The North Platte was deep and swift offering only perilous fords, especially at high water. What was to become the town of Casper was a popular crossing point and soon paying ferries were set up.

The Mormons operated one of these ferries for several years. Eventually a toll bridge was construc-

Glendo Reservoir.

ted near Casper which made the journey much easier.

A number of large dams have been built on the North Platte in Wyoming and over half a million acres are irrigated from the Platte drainage which accounts for a significant part of the State's agricultural production and it provides water for a number of towns. The water in reservoirs behind dams like Seminoe, Alcova, Pathfinder and Glendoe offers wonderful recreational opportunities for boating and fishing. The River also affords habitat for large flocks of migratory waterfowl like geese, ducks and sand hill cranes as well as for endangered species like the whooping crane, the piping plover and the least tern. Inevitably a conflict has arisen between the use of water for irrigation and municipalities and the need to keep a flow for wildlife species. A balance has been reached for the time being, but demands on water supplies continue to grow.

129

Next page :
Around Wheatland in eastern Wyoming crop rotation periodically leaving strips of land fallow has proved an effective means of agriculture.

Water from the Platte River creates a fertile region for agriculture.

The site of Fort Laramie was used as a base for fur trading as early as 1834 and was crucial in Wyoming's early history. It's location at the junction of the North Platte and Laramie Rivers where the first real climb up to South Pass and the Continental Divide began gave it strategic importance. In 1849 when clashes between the local Indian tribes and settlers headed west on the Oregon Trail began to erupt in open warfare the US Army took it over as a headquarters for conducting the Indian Wars and did not abandon it until 1890 when the threat had vanished. It has lost its strategic importance, but has now been restored as a national historic.

RANCHING AND FARMING

Ranching probably plays a more important role in Wyoming life than in any other state. Wyoming never had rich strikes of gold and silver like neighboring Colorado and Montana which brought thousands of miners and their followers so thus there was little to hold any of the stream of settlers passing through with dreams of gold or a more bountiful agricultural environment farther west. After the Civil War with less danger of hostile Indians and dwindling numbers of buffalo, raising cattle became possible and with the advent of the railway in 1867 a market for beef had opened. A supply of cows was needed and there was an overabundance of them in Texas where there was little market for cattle. The problem was transporting them. Fearsome Comanche cavalry had held up settlement in Texas and travel north for decades, but with the Civil War over the army had been able to reduce the danger of Indian attacks. Cattle could be worth ten times as much at the railheads in Kansas as they were in Texas and at the same time people in Wyoming and neighboring states were seeking cattle to begin their own ranching operations.

134

Fall cattle drive on the Padlock ranch.

Cattle cluster near a water hole at the Hideout Ranch.

The time was ripe for the great cattle drives from Texas going as far north as Montana to begin. Stories of these drives have captured the popular imagination internationally and they were by far the biggest cattle drives in the history of the world. The courage, determination and resourcefulness required to overcome the enormous obstacles and the multiple dangers faced were epical. Hostile Indians, crossings of flooded rivers, vast waterless plains, outlaws and stampedes were constant threats. The scale of operations was enormous. Millions of cattle were moved from Texas as far north as Montana and it took thousands of men and tens of thousands of horses to accomplish it. The peak year was 1884 when an estimated 800,000 head crossed the Red River to move north. The riders performed exceptional feats of horsemanship and were mounted on courageous, athletic horses many of which were descended from wild mustang stock. The appeal and romance of the era gave rise to movies like "Red River" and "Lonesome Dove" and has been the subject of countless songs, poems, short stories and books. These cattle drives are responsible for much of the "cowboy" mystique. Certainly there was exaggeration at times in the accounts of those great cattle drive days, but it is often well documented and many of the cowboys truly were heroes. Real events were often stranger than fiction; making hyperbole superfluous.

By the mid 1890s cattle herds were well established in Wyoming. Barbed wire fencing was springing up everywhere. Millions of sheep had also been introduced causing bitter rivalry and sometimes bloody clashes with the cattle men. The railways made access far easier and the Homestead Act of 1862 enabled settlers to acquire land west of the Mississippi free simply by living on it and improving it. The lawless, chaotic, traumatic days of the West were drawing to a close with amazing speed. Custer's Last Stand, the Hole-in-the-wall Gang and the great buffalo herds were only memories. The era of the great drives, like that of the mounted Indian warrior and unrestricted range, glittered brightly for a brief, shining moment in history, flickered and died, but left behind a fascinating legend and a world forever vastly changed.

Raising cattle and sheep in Wyoming is not the same as in the fertile fields of Iowa where less than an acre is needed per cow; in Wyoming it might be more like 100 acres and the land may be cut up by deep gorges, forests and mountains. All along the Rocky Mountain area of the West the transhumance or moving of stock in spring and fall to and from the higher mountains is still vital to the operation of most ranches. They depend on having their stock graze in the high country

Next page :
Three cowboys casting long shadows keep an eye on a herd of Hereford cattle.

during the summer so that they can grow feed for the winter in the lower valleys. Most Wyoming ranches would not be viable without these seasonal movements. Much of the grazing in the high country is in inaccessible places and sometimes in wilderness where all motors are forbidden so that the only practical way to work the cows over these vast areas is still on horseback. Wyoming is a leading state for lamb and wool production, but they are easy targets for a broad range of predators from coyotes to eagles which makes them difficult to raise as they must be watched constantly. It became impossible to find Americans willing to do the difficult, low paid job of caring for sheep so Basque shepherds were brought in a century ago from the Pyrenees and proved outstandingly good at the work which there ancestors had done for many generations. Before long, however, even the Basques decided that there were easier ways to earn a living and only a few old men remain in the business. Now sheep men have turned to Peruvians who are also skilled shepherds in their homeland, but they too are being lured by higher paying jobs in the cities. The result is that herds of sheep in Wyoming are only a fraction of what they were 60 years ago.

The problems faced by the early ranchers were enormous. Predators like wolves, bears and coyotes attacked their animals. The wolves, like the Indians, had depended mainly on the huge herds of buffalo which had disappeared so they naturally turned to the far more vulnerable cattle replacing them on the range. Their depredations took a terrible toll until Government trappers finally managed to get them under control by the 1920s. Cattlemen had to guard their herds vigilantly night and day and keep their rifles at the ready. Lately a larger and fiercer kind of wolf from the Arctic has been introduced in northwest Wyoming again causing time consuming and costly problems for ranchers which are little understood by urban dwellers.

In order to keep cattle in the winter when mountainous areas are covered with deep snow hay and other feed must be harvested in fields at lower altitudes. Since rainfall is usually too sparse to support agriculture in the lower areas irrigation is needed for satisfactory crops. Fortunately the mountains do get a generous amount of snow and rainfall so that streams and rivers flood high in spring with the melting snows. Thus the first priority of ranchers was to divert water from streams and rivers to irrigate their fields which had often been conveniently flattened by glaciers long before. These are the same techniques which enabled agriculture to get started in Egypt and Mesopotamia millennia ago.

Rough winter on Crystal Creek.

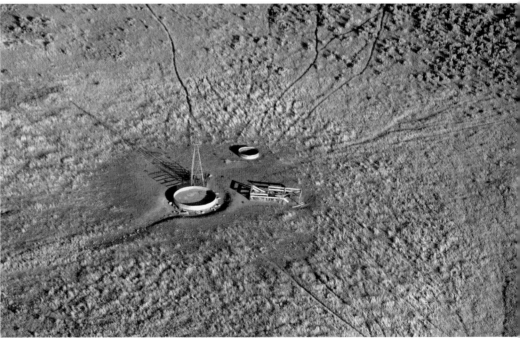

Feedlot near Worland.

Dry water hole near the Red Desert.

The vast open spaces of Wyoming offer ideal habitat for sheep. A century ago, when shepherds were still willing to live a lonely life protecting their flocks far from the amenities and conveniences of our civilization, sheep were far more widespread. Today the coyotes and eagles with a voracious appetite for lamb and mutton remain, but few are prepared to lead a shepherd's life.

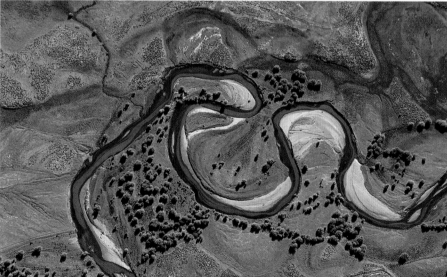

Water is vital for raising livestock in Wyoming and not only for irrigation. Vast areas of the state do have nutritious grass, but it is useless unless the animals have water nearby to drink and they cannot travel the long distances wild animals can to get it. Thus ranchers often build reservoirs to catch runoff or put in windmills to pump water up from shallow wells.

Seasons for growing are short as most of Wyoming's low country is still nearly a mile high, but conditions are excellent for producing high quality grass and alfalfa hay. Some crops like sugar beets and barley are grown successfully in parts of the state, but most agriculture is really tied to feed for livestock. Ranchers therefore are farmers too, though plowing and irrigating the fields hardly has the same exciting appeal as working cattle on horseback. Some big dams have now been built which help control spring runoff, generate hydroelectric power and make large irrigation systems possible.

An important aspect of ranching is tourism and the dude ranch has been a popular attraction in Wyoming for over a century. Dude ranches used to be working ranches where the owners would take paying guests who would join in ranch activities like working cattle as well as just riding, fishing and hunting for the fun of it. Some "dude ranches" have become simply resorts with swimming pools, saunas and horseback riding, but many are still working cattle ranches where they raise and

Headquarters for a modern Crook county ranch.

148

train their own horses as in the early days. These authentic ranches can give visitors the hands on feel of cowboy life.

It is significant that rodeos are very popular in Wyoming and of course the various events are derived from practical ranch work. In the summer weekly rodeos take place in many small towns and are a great social event for the local people. One of America's greatest rodeos, Frontier Days, is held every year in Cheyenne attracting thousands of tourists and many of the world's top riders and horses. The accompanying pageantry is always sumptuous.

Corn field near Sheridan.

Hay field in
Wind River va

Irrigated farmland in
the Bighorn Basin.

WYOMING MINERAL BONANZA, LAND OF ENERGY

Wyoming provides a staggeringly large share of the nation's energy requirements. Something like 25% of the fuel used to generate the nation's electrical energy comes from this state. Today we seem to feel that electricity is almost as necessary as the air we breathe though our founding forefathers, with the exception perhaps of Benjamin Franklin, had no inkling of its future importance. The ability to turn on a light bulb, a cook stove or a computer with a click of the switch is taken totally for granted now, but it requires huge natural resources and enormous effort to keep those circuits we all depend on open.

Though tourism is the biggest employer in Wyoming, mineral extraction provides the largest share of the State's dollar economy and many earn good salaries in the business. Mineral severance taxes make it possible to spare residents from a state income tax. Huge reserves of low sulphur coal from easily accessible open pit mines enable Wyoming to supply over 40% of the nation's

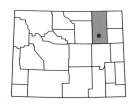

The Black Thunder Coal Mine, second largest in the world.

152

coal and send close to half a billion tons a year to generate much of our country's electric energy, half of which still comes from coal. Even at the present rate of extraction it will take over a century to exhaust our coal reserves. The State is also the second largest producer of natural gas and one of the top exporters of oil and uranium.

Many of us may dither over the environmental damage caused by burning hundreds of millions of years of fossil fuel accumulation in a century or two, but meanwhile our appetite for energy seems insatiable and is growing. Energy availability is closely linked with employment growth and an increase in take home pay which most of us also struggle to achieve. Fortunately Wyoming is also well placed for wind power because of high wind areas with very low population densities and considerable progress has been made already with great potential for the future which will help reduce our dependence on fossil fuels. A significant amount of hydroelectric power is generated in Wyoming, but the potential for an increase from that source is limited.

The Black Thunder coal mine is the second largest in the US and only the neighboring North Antelope Rochelle Mine produces more coal. Black Thunder alone produces 8% of US coal and can load a staggering 25 miles of rail cars per day. Even at that rate of extraction the reserves are thought to be sufficient to last for many decades to come.

Another energy source which could potentially help considerably more in the long run to wean us away from the headlong exploitation of fossil fuels is atomic power. For years France has provided most of its power in this way and is the world's largest exporter of electricity. No serious environmental problems in France are evident as a result. Wyoming has the largest known reserves of uranium of any state and once had a thriving mining business going though, its volume has decreased considerably lately. It may well be that as nuclear technology improves and public attitudes become less emotional our reserves will prove immensely valuable by enabling the generation of cleaner energy.

There are several other useful minerals found in abundance in Wyoming which do not have such a high profile, but make our lives easier. For example we are one of the world's largest suppliers of trona which is our source for baking soda and baking powder as well as being vital in making glass. We are also leaders in supplying bentonite, huge quantities of which are used around the world as a

Oil and gas wells are everywhere in parts of Wyoming.

drilling mud. It has a completely different use as an ingredient of many cosmetics and it is well suited for kitty litter.

Gold and silver do exist in Wyoming, but are no longer mined on a large scale. Atlantic City flourished briefly toward the end of the 19th century, but was abandoned after a few years of feverish activity. Wyoming never had the discoveries of precious metals which brought earlier development to neighboring states like Montana and Colorado.

Relics of Vietnam War long abandoned on the side of Greybull airport.

In Wyoming most of what one normally considers industry is related in one way or another to mining like the oil refinery pictured above though tourism and agriculture are important economic activities. Lumbering was an important industry in the past, but is now relegated to small scale lumber mills and log home manufacture. Many homes are heated by firewood found locally and ranchers often use posts and poles they cut themselves or bought from neighbors.

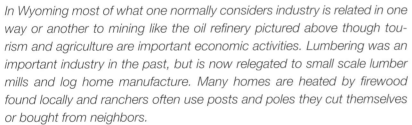

As we face the growing necessity to reduce our dependence on fossil fuels for the generation of electricity we have turned more and more toward cleaner means of creating energy like water, solar and wind power. Wyoming has the advantage of strong winds blowing comparatively steadily at high altitudes and of large, uninhabited areas where huge windmills can be installed. The industry is still in its infancy and remains controversial because of the high cost of construction and alleged adverse environmental and aesthetic impacts. This may change as the technology improves and the need to shun fossil fuels becomes more dire.

Wind mill fields on Foote Creek Rim.

CHEYENNE, STATE CAPITAL

Cheyenne is Wyoming's capital and largest city. The population of the greater metropolitan area is nearly 100,000. Cheyenne got its real start in 1867 when the transcontinental railway reached there and the town became an important center for the surrounding area. It was named after one of the most important Plains Indian tribes who roamed through this part of the state. In 1869 the Territorial Government had the distinction of being the first part of our country to give women the right to vote. Wyoming was also the first to have a woman governor and a woman justice of the peace. In part at least this must have been a tribute to the important role women have played in the settlement and development of the state.

In the early years the Wyoming Stock Growers' Association with headquarters in Cheyenne was really the de facto government and they set many of the laws to suit their needs. A crisis came with the fearsome blizzards of 1886 when a large percentage of the cattle in Wyoming and neighboring

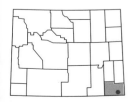

Downtown Cheyenne.

162

states died of starvation and exposure. The range had become overstocked and overgrazed in the 20 years since the first great cattle drives had started coming up from Texas and the herds had thrived and multiplied too well in Wyoming and neighboring states. The result was that after the great die off many cowboys were thrown out of work and some tried to set up their own small ranches with the help of the Homestead Act which enabled them to acquire title to tracts of land free

the smaller homesteaders and open up the land for the big ranches again. Apparently they intended to kill a number of the smaller ranchers they accused of rustling cattle. The group ran into stiff resistance and was eventually surrounded and besieged at the TA Ranch by the sheriff of Buffalo and a posse he had raised. The US Army was called in by the Association to rescue the gunmen they had sent and most of the expedition was returned to Cheyenne under Army guard though a number of men on both si-

simply by living on it and improving it. Allegedly some of them tried to start their own herds with cattle stolen from the large ranches and dangerous tensions arose.

This was the period of the Johnson County War when gunmen from Texas were hired by the Stock Growers to drive out

des were killed in the fighting before the soldiers arrived. The members of the dubious Stock Growers expedition were returned to Cheyenne and nominally jailed awaiting sentencing which never occurred and eventually charges were dropped. Resentment over the affair smoldered for generations.

CHEYENNE FRONTIER DAYS

Cheyenne is world famous for hosting the Frontier Days Rodeo, the largest outdoor rodeo in the world which began in 1897. It is a ten day affair attracting hundreds of thousands of visitors from around the world and including some of the best riders and livestock to be found anywhere. The pageantry is sumptuous with picturesque parades and since 1953 a breathtaking aerobatic performance from the United States Air Force Thunderbirds stationed nearby.

Today Cheyenne is an attractive city with a low crime rate and good living conditions. Many residents are employed in some aspect of the State Government or by the US Forest Service and some work at the nearby Warren Air Force Base which is one of our most important places for strategic missiles.

The rich pageantry surrounding the rodeo itself including parades and concerts helps make this event a grand old tradition celebrating the best of Western culture and a way of life which helped make America the great country it is.

WYOMING TOWNS

Sheridan is located at the base of the Bighorn Mountains near the border of Montana on the edge of the Great Plains. It has a comparatively mild climate and is surrounded by some of Wyoming's best agricultural land. Members of the British aristocracy settled near here early in the town's history and some of them began raising horses for the British Cavalry through the 1800s and until the early 1900s.

Today it is a great center for polo and there is an active equestrian group. The town also hosts a well known rodeo which attracts top riders. Many of the last battles of the Indian wars were fought in the area including Custer's stunning defeat at the Battle of the Little Bighorn. Sheridan rates high for its quality of life and, like Laramie, is considered a good place to retire.

Rock Springs is another town which got its start supporting the transcontinental railway. Coal mines nearby were a convenient source for fuel for the locomotive engines of the time which left a plume of smoke behind as they steamed across

Sheridan.

172

Rock Springs.

the nation and stokers kept shoveling more coal into the burners. Rock Springs, like Gillette, is near rich sources of oil and natural gas which has attracted many to the city. There is a dark incident in the past where perhaps the worst race riot in American history occurred. Chinese miners had been brought in to mine coal for the railway and they were prepared to work for lower pay than those of European origin, throwing them out of work. Resentment reached such a fever pitch that in 1895 the white miners went on the rampage and killed dozens of Chinese so that the US Army had to be brought in to quell the riots. Since that time the town has had its vicissitudes including a corrupt local government in the 1970s, but it has overcome these problems and is an attractive place to live amid beautiful scenery and with a thriving economy thanks to oil and natural gas reserves nearby.

Dubois is a picturesque little town of a thousand people in a remote corner of Wyoming 75 miles from the nearest other town. It is surrounded by vast national forests with exceptional opportunities for hiking, horseback riding, hunting and fishing. Lumbering used to be important, but tourism is the main activity now and some of Wyoming's oldest and best known dude ranches are in the area.

Dubois.

Casper got its start as a place to cross the North Platte River for travelers on the Oregon Trail. First there were ferries and later a toll bridge which greatly facilitated travel. After Casper the Oregon Trail leaves the Platte and heads up the Sweetwater to South Pass and the Red Desert.

The Historic Trails Interpretive Center in Casper recreates the history of those early times in detail. Today one can retrace part of the old trail for hours or even days in horse drawn wagons built like those which carried a half a million immigrants over the Rockies in the fifty years before the completion of the railway in 1868.

The Bridge at Battle Creek Station near Casper has a bloody history as Indian tribes like the Sioux, the Cheyenne and the Arapahoe were beginning to be seriously impacted by the wagon trains. Streams of settlers passing through were killing all the game for miles around their route as they were suffering badly for food supplies since they were limited as to what they could carry. Finally the Indians, seeing the game they depended on in their traditional hunting grounds decimated and fearing starvation themselves, lost their patience and decided to destroy this crucial bridge. Over a thousand warriors participated in the attack on the bridge which was defended by a detachment of soldiers. The Indians wiped out a small wagon train and managed to kill several dozen soldiers, but did not take the bridge which was defended with a howitzer from the fort overlooking the bridge. About sixty warriors died and many were wounded. Among the soldiers killed was a gallant officer called Caspar Collins and the town of Casper was named after him. They did not use his last name because there was already a Ft. Collins in Colorado named after his father. The change in spelling from Caspar to Casper was due to a clerk's error.

Today Casper is the second largest city in Wyoming with a population of about 55,000 and is the State's oil capital as well as being a supply center for the surrounding ranches. In the 1890s when oil was just starting to become a precious commodity the Salt Creek Oil Field was discovered just north of Casper which was the nearest railhead. As early as 1895 a refinery was operating there and oil has been the driving force of the economy ever since. Lately activity has been stepping up for oil exploration as consumption increases and our foreign supplies seem more precarious.

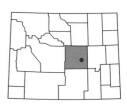

Casper.

While the State of Wyoming is our top energy producer, the town of Gillette can claim the title of the "energy capital of the world" with considerable justification. Gillette actually has the goods at its doorstep in the form of the largest open pit, low sulphur coal mines in the world not to mention coal bed methane gas and oil. The town has a population of about 30,000 residents and has had to struggle with the problem of a rapid influx of people caused by the energy boom in a comparatively short time. It is a classic example of the problems which can be caused in a boom town where social patterns change suddenly with an influx of outsiders who often have totally different backgrounds and philosophies. Family life is often disrupted and the Newcomers sometimes do not feel the same dedication to the long term health of the community. It is a syndrome oft repeated in the West since the California Gold Rush of 1849 and it takes time to heal. The increased wealth can be as much of a curse as a benefit.

177

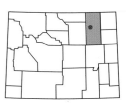

Gillette.

Cody evokes the spirit of the old West more effectively than any other town and is steeped in Western folklore. It is named for its founder, Colonel "Buffalo Bill" Cody, that expert army scout, Pony Express rider, buffalo hunter and showman par excellence who personifies the cowboy mystique. His Wild West shows captivated crowds from the Mississippi to Eastern Europe and enthralled millions with the exotic charm and excitement of the American Frontier. He persuaded his friend, President Theodore Roosevelt, to facilitate the building of a dam on the nearby Shoshone River, making possible a hydroelectric plant and irrigation of the surrounding area which greatly stimulated the economy. Colonel Cody also built the still operating Irma Hotel, named for one of his daughters, which exudes the atmosphere of the past.

The Buffalo Bill Historical Center includes a vast number of exhibits ranging from the wildlife of the area to Western Art and cultural history. Visitors could spend days here studying these exceptional artifacts and paintings which are beautifully displayed and described to bring our history alive. The Old West Trail Town contains many painstakingly reconstructed buildings from pioneer days which give the feel of those old days. The spirit of the West is also manifested in Cody by the rodeos taking place there every evening in the summer.

The only passage to Yellowstone Park on its eastern side passes through Cody and brings many tourists to the town so that tourism is by far the most important activity.

Laramie.

181

Riverton.

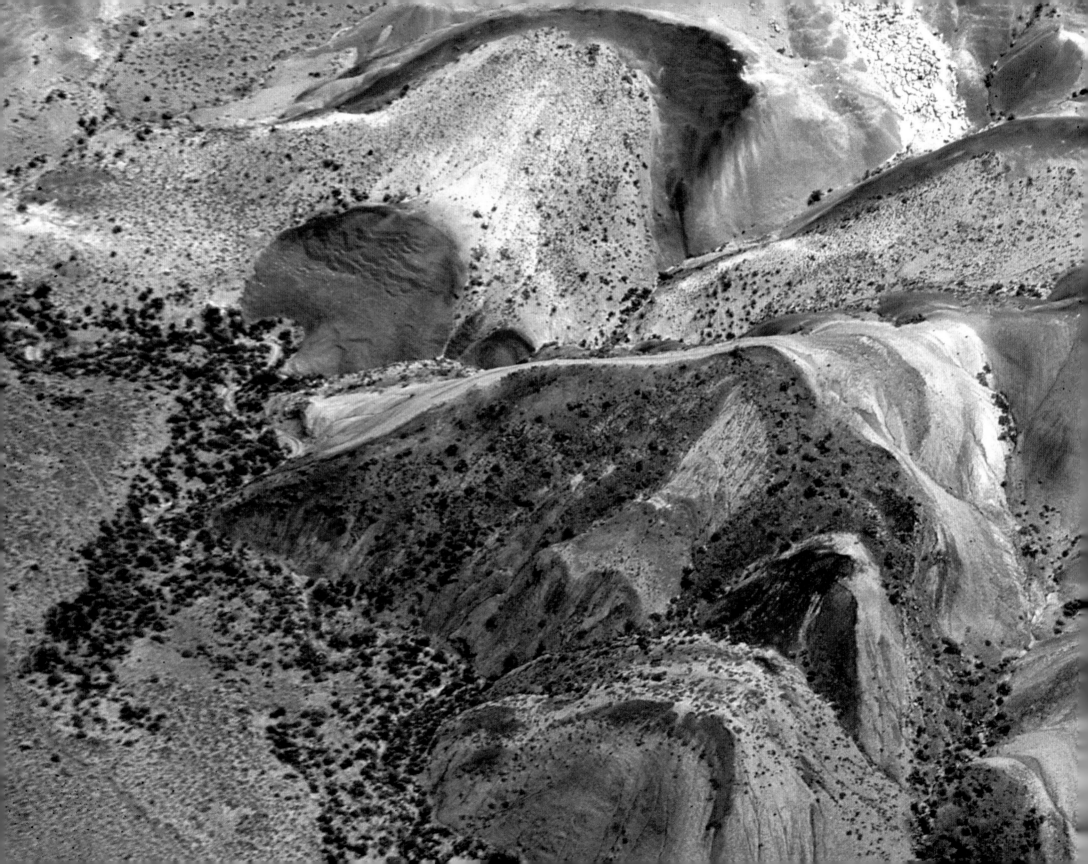

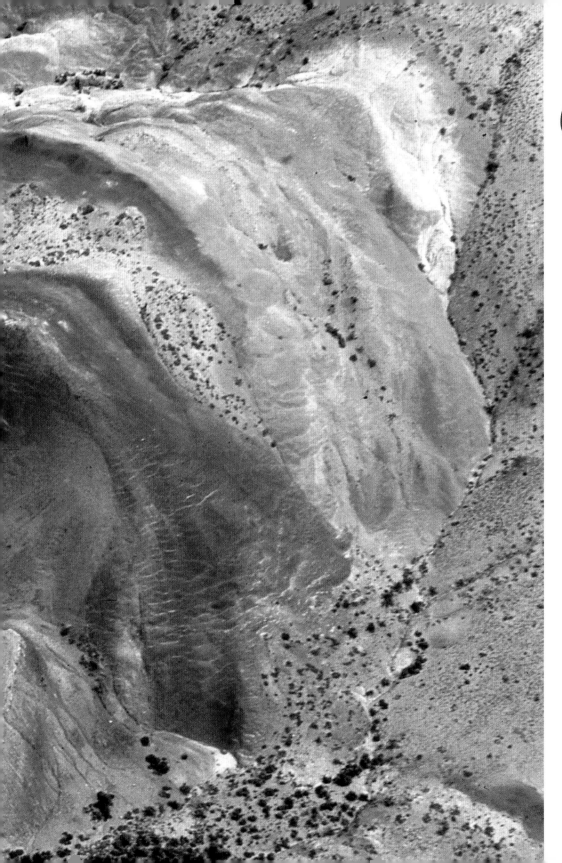

WYOMING, LAND OF CONTRASTS

Simply saying that the geology of Wyoming is spectacular and complex is a ridiculous understatement for words are totally inadequate as the pictures in this book so vividly demonstrate. Brilliant geologists have spent their lives puzzling out the secrets of how this dramatic landscape was created and still have much to learn. We are not merely looking at millions of years of history, but billions. The chaotic turmoil of gigantic forces like volcanic eruptions, the movement of glaciers and the earth's shifting tectonic plates often show clearly on the surface. The flat and fertile plains of Kansas reveal little of the past, but here geology is evident in all its awesome glory. A disproportionate number of Wyoming natives have been inspired to become geologists by the state's spectacular topography.

Countless volumes have been written about Wyoming's geology, most of it unintelligible to the layman. We give only a short overview here to help

It took titanic natural forces and years of erosion to create this fantastic topography near Greybull.

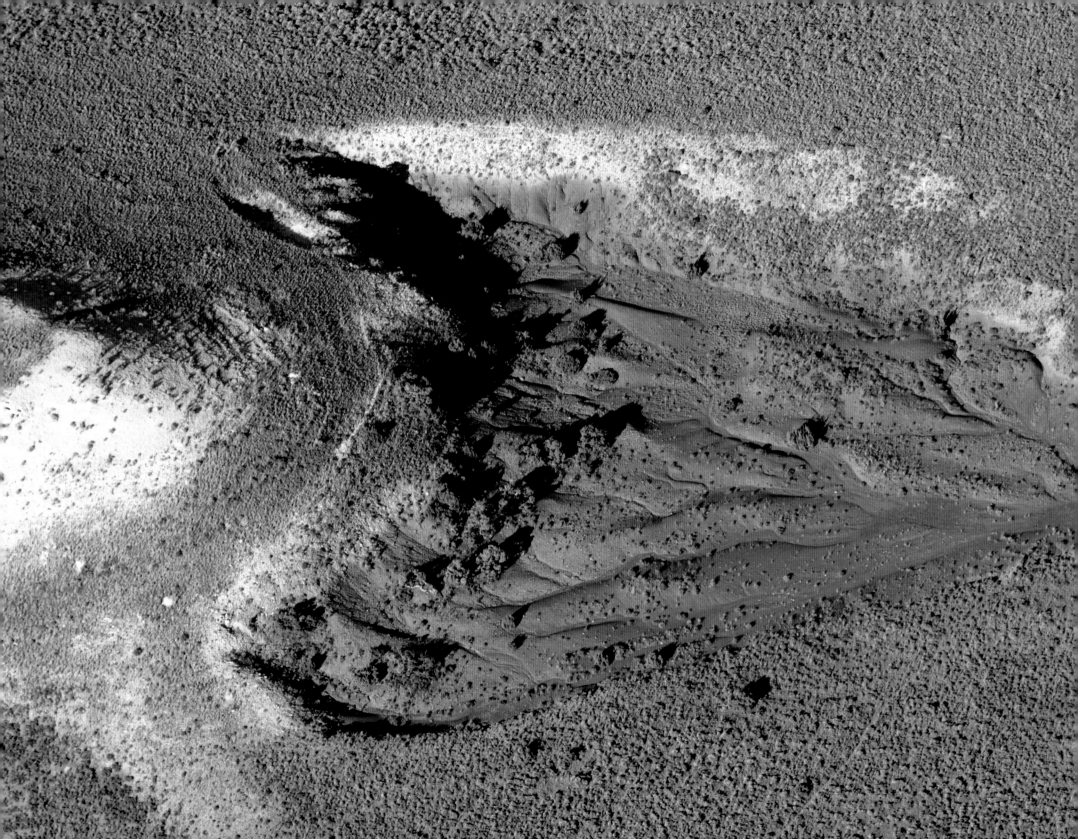

the reader understand the area's history and present day developments. In the Paleozoic Era, several hundred million years ago, much of the state was under an ocean and fossils like shark teeth are still found from this period. In the more recent Cenozoic Era, 38-65 million years ago, Wyoming was covered with thick, sub-tropical swamps with lush vegetation and deciduous trees.

This is why today there are such rich supplies of fossil fuels; oil, natural gas and almost half the coal reserves in the US. This incredible wealth is now the most important single driving force of the state's economy.

It is a fascinating place for paleontologists as well. Fossils of dinosaurs, titanathirs, the ancestors of the horse and countless other animals, reptiles, fish, plants and trees have been found. Rock hounds have a happy hunting ground here too as there are agates, beautiful petrified wood, gold and many other treasures lurking in stream beds, cut banks, outcroppings of rock or even on the open prairie.

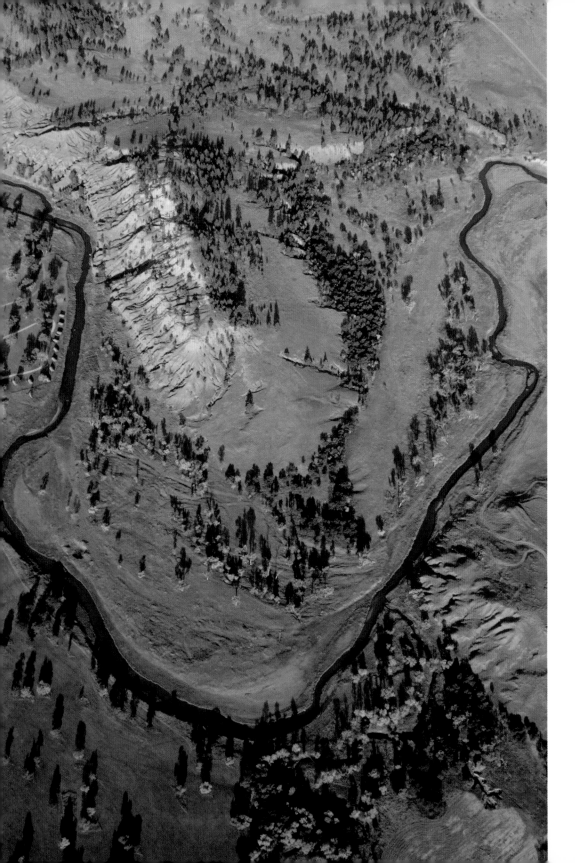

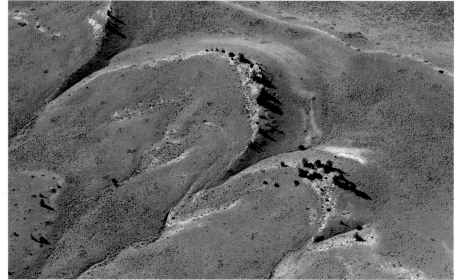

Wyoming is not only one of our largest states; it also has some of the most varied topography. The vast expanses of the Great Plains end here in Wyoming where they meet the mountains and soon after entering the state one can begin to see the exciting glimmer of snowcapped mountains beckoning the traveler on. Many distinct mountain ranges cut up the state and the Continental Divide passes right through it from north to south. Places like the Red Desert and the Badlands near Dubois are reminiscent of Arizona's Monument Valley or Bryce Canyon National Park.

The reddish tinges of iron oxide on barren hillsides give way to streaks of green from copper and there are weird formations from titanic volcanic upheavals followed by millennia of erosion from wind and water. Just a few miles away from the Dubois Badlands the verdant hillsides of the Absarokas and the Wind Rivers take over the scene. At the western end of the state one finds the idyllic, unspoiled valley of Jackson Hole with the Tetons towering above and the Snake River winding below. Toward the eastern end are the great chasms left by the accelerating extraction of millions of tons of low sulphur coal which seems to be indispensable in satisfying our insatiable appetite for energy. Fortunately Wyoming is still big enough to fill our aesthetic need for unspoiled nature and our desire for an easier life, but the conflicts become more pressing.

Wyoming's climate offers some sharply contrasting conditions. Parts of the Great Basin receive less than 5 inches of precipitation in some years and are virtually desert where even cactus does not flourish. Within sight of these dry areas some mountain ranges can be smothered under 200 inches of snow. The combination of powdery snow and the same strong winds which power the windmills so effectively make for deep, impassable drifts in places and often complicate traffic in winter despite the construction of many miles of snow fence. Temperatures often vary as much as 50 degrees Fahrenheit from day to night. The weather in the mountains is usually beautiful through the early fall, but sometimes a late September snowstorm can dump 2 or 3 feet of snow on hunting camps so that horses are struggling up to their bellies and the wild animals make tracks for lower country. Even in August a sudden snow can surprise a pack trip. Vegetable gardens in the high country sometimes only have 60 frost free days. A storm in the mountains can cause serious flash floods in one valley while a valley ten miles away remains dry.

The spirit of the pioneers is still strong in those who spend their lives in this rugged, harsh landscape.

Thank you so much to Dave STINSON the "big chief pilot" but also Tim SHELL, Mark DONAHUE
Ken OVERFIELD, Steve SHAFFER from SKY AVIATION,
Doniv FELTNER over Cheyenne and Justin STRUB over Gillette
Many thanks to my friends Severine and Robert Murdoch who help me a lot since 20 years.
Claude Poulet

My special thanks go to my wife, Mel, whose advice, editing and tireless proof reading were of indispensable help. The unique aerial photographs of Claude Poulet, so painstakingly assembled flying in a small plane, have been an inspiration in writing the text. I also give my heartfelt thanks to my friend and fellow Yalie, Laton McCartney, for his eloquent introduction.
Bayard Fox

Bibiography
American Colonies – by Alan Taylor
The Mustangs – J. Frank Dobie
Fremont Country Wyoming: A Pictorial History – by Loren Jost
Alpine Sentinels – by Tony Taylor
The Sheep Eaters of Yellowstone Park – by Lawrence L. Loendorf and Nancy Medaris Stone
Washakie: Chief of the Shoshones – by Grace Raymond Hebard
People of the Wind River – Henry E. Stamm, IV
For Everything There Is a Season – by Frank C. Craighead, Jr.
Sagebrush Country – by Ronald J. Taylor
Western Trees – by George A. Petrides and Olivia Petrides
Wind River Country – Website
The Horse in Blackfoot Indian Culture – by John Ewers
In Search of Butch Cassidy – by Larry Pointer
Climbing and Hiking in the Wind River Mountains – by Joe Kelsey
Rising from the Plains – by John McPhee
Wikepedia
Across the Great Divide – Laton McCartney
www.wyomingtalesandtrails.com